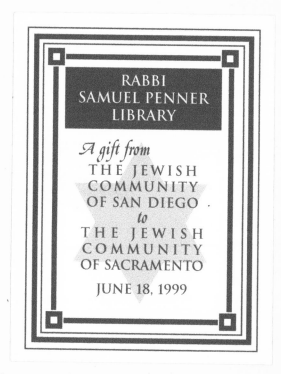

Judaism for Today

JEWISH THOUGHTS FOR CONTEMPORARY
JEWISH YOUTH

JUDAISM FOR TODAY

Jewish Thoughts
for Contemporary Jewish Youth

ABRAHAM CRONBACH

INTRODUCTION BY JOHN HAYNES HOLMES

BOOKMAN ASSOCIATES   NEW YORK

TO

NELSON GLUECK

PRESIDENT OF THE HEBREW UNION COLLEGE-
JEWISH INSTITUTE OF RELIGION IN TOKEN OF
THE AUTHOR'S PROFOUND ESTEEM

Contents

Introduction

I AM writing this Foreword, or Introduction, to Dr. Cronbach's volume, as first of all a tribute to the author. In the half-century of our friendship, I have found in this distinguished teacher a man as brave as he is learned. He has lived through terrific times—has seen his society and culture brought more than once to the very verge of ruin. What we have all suffered in this tragic hour, the Jews have suffered in magnified measure, till death itself became to them a boon. But the rabbis and their people neither faltered nor failed. Amid whatsoever diffusion of opinion, these heroic souls stood firm in their faith, and thus achieved again the survival of their people. High on this roll of honor stands Dr. Cronbach, happily alive to see the vindication of his fellow-Jews.

This book is what Jews and Christians alike have long been looking for—a statement, in simple yet vivid terms, of the religious thought of Judaism. The author, in true humility of spirit, describes his work as written for "Jewish Youth." So it is!— but quite as much also for Jews of all ages, young and old together. In the same way, he speaks of his book as a collection of "Jewish Thoughts." This implies a casual gathering of occasional ideas, scattered in anthology-style under headings of great or little interest. But Dr. Cronbach, in this description of his work, is unjust both to himself and his own faith. This book is a genuine piece of scholarship. It is learning without pedantry, clarity divorced of confusion. In its own modest way, it is at once a carefully sustained theological argument and a true specimen of literary art. What we have here is the fruitage of Dr. Cronbach's many years of study, simply stated, yet by his abundant labors and highly disciplined thought transformed into a veritable testament of wisdom.

Dr. Cronbach begins his argument with a careful and judicious distinction between "religion" and "religions." The temptation of every faith—Christianity, for example—is to claim all religion for itself. Its teaching is described as uniquely inspired and thus infallible. All other so-called religions are presented as frauds and heresies, and therefore to be cast away as so much theological rubbish. But Dr. Cronbach is guilty of no such error. All religions, he declares, have their share of truth, and therefore their measure of sanctity. Dr. Cronbach sets his own religion, where it properly belongs, as one among the various religions of mankind, which, flowing like a river of many waters, attains at last that "one vast ocean of accord" which is the universal whole. In the case of Judaism, its content of religion is seen to be largely ethical, and in this sense makes clear its unique contribution to the deposits of the spirit. "Reverence for human personality, that can be our religion," writes Dr. Cronbach, "a religion which holds the solution of some of our gravest problems."

This general depiction of religion as humanistic, or ethical, in character, leads at once to a profound and beautiful presentation of the idea of God and the reality of his presence among men. This presence reveals itself in one of two ways—one by report, and the other by experience. The God who appears as "something reported" is more or less remote, and is reached only by processes of indirection. This is where our scriptures and prophecies and testaments come in as means of reaching a deity, who, by his very nature, is more or less unattainable. But the God of experience is with us as a very part of our eternal being. We see him and feel him as our own, and therewith a personal presence within our very souls. We need no intermediary to bring his revelation to our enjoyment and use. He is ours by our own right. At the heart of this experience lies the practice of prayer, and its immediacy with God. It is here, in his distinction between God as reported and God as experienced, that Dr. Cronbach is at his best. This is the genius of the Jews made clear.

Following these basic chapters comes naturally the detached discussion of familiar topics—the law of righteousness which is Judaism's supreme contribution to history, social idealism, Jewish and Christian interrelations, pacifism, and immortality. Of these arguments in the purely religious field, I am myself most deeply moved by the chapter on pacifism, which I rate as the clearest, bravest, and most uncompromising treatment of this theme I have ever read—an indispensable consideration of this difficult and dangerous problem. But the most important and significant chapter of this book is the one on "life everlasting." For some reason I have never rightly understood, the attitude of the Jews toward the question of immortality has not seldom been unsatisfactory—the weakest joint in Israel's armor! But Dr. Cronbach's discussion of this loftiest ideal of the spirit is superbly done, and thus goes far toward redeeming this fundamental aspect of religious thought.

I welcome this opportunity of presenting Dr. Cronbach's work to the many readers who are waiting his word, among Jews and Christians alike. Nobody realizes the inadequacy of this introduction more than I. But if it opens the doorway into the author's able mind by so much as a few inches, I shall be content, for such beginning must follow through to the very end. It is in this regard that I stand immeasurably indebted to my old friend and comrade for allowing me to serve him in this happy way. With confidence and cheer, I say Amen, and again Amen, to the discussion which impatiently awaits my retirement from the scene.

JOHN HAYNES HOLMES

Minister Emeritus
The Community Church
of New York

CHAPTER ONE

Religion

MAKING THE READER acquainted with ancient Jewish teachings is not the prime object of this book. Our main purpose will be that of aiding the reader in the solution of his or her own problems. Some of our problems are akin to those of long ago. Our solutions will, in some instances, resemble those of long ago. Sometimes our solutions and those of long ago will differ. Looking at those ancient solutions and judging wherein they do or do not meet our needs of today should aid us as we cope with our own bewilderments.

Our study is to range within the sphere of religion. The word "religion" has been applied to a large variety of phenomena. Building hospitals for the indigent sick has been an act of religion; burning heretics at the stake has also been an act of religion. Religion has manifested itself in lives of humility and saintliness; it has also manifested itself in pomposities, bigotries, and persecutions. Religion has preached and even practiced the returning of good for evil; it has also lent itself to quarreling over trivialities of ritual. Religion has shown itself a promoter of learning; at other times, it has fostered ignorance and superstition. Religion has cultivated the beautiful; at other times, it has courted the ugly. Our own Judaism has had its gentle Hillel; it has also had its excommunicators of Spinoza. Christianity has produced its kindly Saint Francis; it has also produced its Crusaders who, on their way through Europe, laid a trail of rapine and massacre. How shall we account for these disparities?

1. THE NATURE OF THE WORD

The fact that the word "religion" can label such a broad diversity should not surprise us. This lurks in the nature of language itself. Most words are ever acquiring new and added meanings. Webster's Unabridged Dictionary offers eighteen definitions for the word "watch," fourteen for the word "star," eighteen for the word "carriage," thirty-six for the word "head," and forty-one for the word "run." Science, which would be utterly thwarted by such motility of language, contrives its polysyllabic words of Greek derivation—such terms as "apotropaic," "haplography," "sphygmograph," "epexegetical"—"jaw-breakers," we call them—words too involved to enter people's everyday vocabulary where meanings rapidly multiply as words pass from mouth to mouth.

Nor is this all. Some words affect us pleasantly, and some affect us unpleasantly. Examples of the former are: "fragrance," "beauty," "freedom." Examples of the latter are: "rat," "rotten," "crank." When words affect us pleasantly, we attach them only to persons, objects, and actions that affect us pleasantly. The converse holds with terms which we find disagreeable. Thus we speak of a "fragrant" memory or of a "beautiful" character; while someone whose conduct outrages us, we stigmatize as a "rat" or as "rotten." We use the pleasant words for that which we would praise, and the repellent words when our object is to condemn.

Our previous experiences, especially childhood experiences, associated with a word, determine whether that word will prove gratifying or displeasing. The word "religion" is no exception. That word serves not merely to label; it serves likewise to laud or to brand. Some people love the word and apply it only to that which they esteem. The reverse prevails with those for whom the word has become offensive. We hear people say: "Witch-baiting, I would hardly call religion." "The charity he gave, was not that the finest kind of religion?" "Religion comforts and strengthens." "To do good, that is my religion." The following would illustrate the opposite: "The purpose of religion is to make people submissive to exploitation." "Religion is nothing but humbug." "Fighting the discoveries of Galileo, Darwin, Wellhausen, Freud—there you have samples of religion." "Kindness is not religion; kindness is ethics."

2. RELIGIONIZING AND DERELIGIONIZING

People for whom the connotation of the word "religion" is favorable tend to reserve the word for that which impresses them as supremely important and which evokes their reverence. This gives rise to the processes of religionizing and dereligionizing. Religionizing means the introduction of the new; *de*religionizing means the discarding of the old. When, for instance, the Central Conference of American Rabbis adopted resolutions endorsing the unionization of labor, the Americanization of the immigrant, pensions for the aged, aid to dependent children, government subvention of housing for the needy, the abolition of child labor, and the like, they religionized those concerns. Decades earlier, Jewish worship religionized the music of the organ; organ music had previously been debarred. Rabbis, pastors, and others connected with synagogues and churches are, in some places, beginning to counsel people with regard to marriage, thus religionizing that species of guidance. The discussions now prevalent about the connection between religion and mental health indicate a wish to religionize some forms of psychiatry. Centuries ago, the Jews adopted the Feast of Lots and the Feast of Dedication, thereby religionizing those observances. About the year 1810, liberal Jews religionized the ceremony of confirmation. In some quarters today, both Christian and Jewish, there has developed a religionizing of pacifism just as, ages ago, there emerged a religionizing of war. Into religion, new ideas and new practices are constantly entering. Often these new ideas and practices existed outside of religion before they became part of religion. But, whether they were copied by some religion or invented by some religion, they exemplify religionizing. To things which people intensely favor, they append the word "religion"—provided the word itself meets with their favor. Thus do new elements become linked with that which had previously acquired religious significance.

Alongside of religionizing, there runs the counter-process of *de*religionizing. Christianity which, long ago, dereligionized the belief that the sun moves over the earth, is now struggling to dereligionize the church's segregation of Negroes. Reform Judaism has dereligionized the ritual covering of the head as well as the second day of the holidays. Many Jewish persons have abandoned—that is to say, dereligionized—the traditional restrictions of diet; likewise the seven-day period of mourning. Some have even dereligionized the reciting of the prayer in memory of the dead. The Mormons once religionized, and subsequently dereligionized, polygamy. We noticed how a usage which becomes religionized may, in some cases, have existed outside of religion before the religionizing took place. By contrast, the practices which become dereligionized often disappear; often, but not always. Medicine, which was once a religious institution, continues as a secular institution. Similarly art, law, and education survive in their secular form long after they have withdrawn from religious auspices.

Religionizing and *de*religionizing mark also the career of the individual. There are those who, in their ideals and their conduct, have religionized truthfulness, friendliness, and benevolence. There are also those who, while not treating those qualities with any disdain, prefer to identify their religion with the lighting of candles, the reading of the prayer book, visiting the cemetery, or advancing the State of Israel in Palestine. Each one's religion issues from his or her personal choice. Each must elect the values which he or she will vest with sanctity and paramount importance.

3. RELIGION, SCIENCE, ART

Not the least of our quandaries will be that of adjusting our religious interests to our scientific interests. Opposition to science became religionized centuries ago. The dereligionizing of that opposition has not yet become universal. The clear, coherent, and responsible thinking which science demands is an arduous task. That multitudes should long for exemption from that burden was inevitable. We need not be astonished that people should so crave escape from the irksomeness of scientific thought as to religionize that escape. If, however, we choose to religionize truthfulness, then every obstruction to scientific thinking becomes alien to our outlook.

The various movements labeled "religious" have displayed, alongside of their antipathy to science, yet another trait, a totally different trait. That other trait has been devotion to art. Art became religionized at the dawn of history. Though, in our own generation, art has grown extensively secularized, a vast amount of art still remains sacred. Not a little of the architecture, sculpture, painting, music, and poetry cherished and cultivated today, originated in religious circles, utilizes religious themes, and subserves religious purposes.

Though we have long heard of a conflict between religion and science, no one has ever dreamed of a conflict between art and science. Not a few people for whom "religion" is a term of stigma, enjoy the poetry of Dante, Goethe, and Milton—yes, even that of the Bible. They glory in the architecture of Saint Peter's Cathedral or Westminster Abbey or Temple Emanu-El, and thrill at the sacred music in the repertoires of the great choruses and orchestras. The artistic side of religion and the anti-scientific side of religion are, in all events, separate and distinct.

Consider also the element of respect for human personality, religionized by the prophets of the Old Testament, extolled by all cults and, in the name of religion, even practiced by some individuals and groups. What do we mean by respect for human personality? There are two ways in which people can be treated. We can view them as things to be used, as means for our own ends, as tools for our own purposes. Sometimes we use people, if in no other way, at least for the coddling of our Ego. Those of us who hunger for flattery value people chiefly as mouthpieces of that flattery, betraying ourselves by our very idiom, "I have no *use* for him," when the flattery is not forthcoming. That is one manner in which we can react. The other way consists in treating people not as means toward ends but as ends in themselves, not as things but as beings like ourselves, beings whom we can understand and appreciate and with whom we can enter into cooperation. The latter attitude constitutes respect for human personality.

We might raise the question whether the artistic side of religion and respect for human personality are not closely akin. There is a beauty of architecture, sculpture, painting, music, poetry. May there not also be a beauty of human relationships? Familiar is the phrase, "the beauty of holiness." There is indeed a beauty of holiness. Love, devotion, consecration, loyalty possess beauty in a superlative degree.

Nor is artistic beauty the highest form of beauty. What painting is there which has ever attained the beauty of an exquisite landscape, where the beauty of dawn passes into the beauty of noontide, the beauty of noontide into that of the dusk, the beauty of summer into that of autumn, the beauty of autumn into that of winter, and where the beauty of winter yields to the beauty of spring? In their responses to the beauties of nature, few religions have been backward. Religious song, poetry, and painting brim with ecstasy when describing nature's loveliness.

Whether we regard the beauties of human relationships as akin to those of art or akin to those of nature, it suffices that the beauty is there. The urge in the human mind which led to the religionizing of beauty, seen and heard, might well be identical with the urge which led to the religionizing of reverence for human personality.

Reverence for human personality—that can be our religion. That can be, for us, the meaning of God. Here is a religion which at no point collides with science. Here also is a religion which holds the solutions of some of our gravest problems.

CHAPTER TWO

God

GOD IS A THEME of moment to everyone interested in religion. The word occurs constantly in prayer. It comes up repeatedly in religious discussion. The question whether or not God exists has been debated by not a few of us at some time in our lives.

1. THE EXPERIENCED VERSUS THE REPORTED

It is important to notice that the word "God" does not always carry the same meaning. The word means one thing when people argue. It means another thing when people pray. The difference rests upon the fact that, at times, the word "God" refers to something reported; at other times, to something which people experience. The difference is easy to grasp. The experienced is that which is present; the reported is that which is not present. The canals on Mars, the tides in the Bay of Fundy, or the events of the Stone Age illustrate things reported. A landscape at which we are looking, music to which we are listening, or the friend with whom we are conversing illustrate something experienced. When people speak of God as the creator of the world, the dispenser of rain, the director of historical events, or as One who rewards and punishes, then is God a reported God. How different when people testify to the "inner light," to "God within one's heart," or to "His presence within the soul"! Then is God not something about which one hears or reads. God is then an experience.

What is that experience? It is the experience of *redemption*. By redemption, we understand nothing occult, mysterious, or supernatural. By redemption, we mean simply the good in a world otherwise gloomed with woe. Sorrow and suffering, disappointment and defeat beset every life. Yet we experience not only pain; we experience also relief from pain. The world contains tribulation; but it also contains joy. When people utter the word "God," it is to this healing, consolation, deliverance, restoration that they commonly allude. The word "God" serves, in such cases, not as a label like "house," "boy," "dollar." It functions more like "beautiful," "lovely," "precious," "paragon," "perfection"—words which do not label something but which manifest our feelings. The usage, moreover, becomes non-literal. We speak of God as a Heavenly Father, a Savior, a Helper, a Protector, a Friend. These appellatives bear a super-literal import. We glory in *Freedom on her mountain height* and in *Columbia, the gem of the ocean.* We learn that the sun *attracts* the earth and that water *seeks* its lowest level or that the *upsurge* of public opinion forced the President to take certain *steps.* The non-literal use of language is as extensive as its literal use. Why should religion call for an exception?

Those words, "father," "savior," "helper," "protector," "friend," signify redemption in its highest form. They derive from redemption in our human relationships. Our most dismal woes are due to our collisions with other human beings; hatred and strife rank among the worst of our disasters. Correspondingly, love and peace and reverence for human personality constitute the most precious of our deliverances. How inevitable that those great moments in our lives should overshadow our religious vocabulary! In short, behind such terms as "Father," "Savior," "Helper," "Protector," "Friend," stands redemption, the supreme fact of the universe. Redemption is what people, at times of devoutness, have in mind when they invoke God. For this they yearn when they yearn for God. This they need when they need God. This they find when they find God.

It is far otherwise when people, adjourning prayer and edification, engage in religious debates and arguments. Then the word

"God" refers no longer to something which they experience. It then refers to something reported. "God" is then no longer a word which acclaims; it gets to be a word which labels. Nor does it function any longer non-literally. At such moments, people name God literally the Creator of the world, the Prime Mover, the Cause of various happenings, the Rewarder and Punisher. And this reported God is the God denied by the atheist and challenged by modern science. The God of experience is like anything else we experience. To anything we experience, contradiction and denial have no applicability.

Not the God of experience but the God of report is the topic of the interminable discussion why, if God is good, there should be, in the world, so much misery; and why, if God rewards and punishes, do the righteous suffer and the wicked prosper. With reference to the God of experience, these questions lack all relevance. From the world's good, the God of experience does not stand separate. The God of experience is identical with that good. In the religion of experience, God does not send the good or withhold the good. God *is* the good.

2. THE PROBLEM OF EVIL

As for the evil in the world, that question belongs not so much to religion as to philosophy. Philosophically speaking, bad and good are but the obverse and the reverse of the same coin. Bad and good go inseparably together. The same laws of nature that produce the good produce also the bad. Our bodies, just because they are capable of thought, accomplishment, joy, beauty, love, are likewise susceptible to disease, distortion, dementia, despair. Our capabilities require complexity of structure; and the greater the complexity, the greater the possibility of disorder and agony. Animals suffer less than human beings, plants less than animals, and rocks and metals suffer not at all; the less the complexity, the less the pain. We might truthfully assert that everything bad in the world is but the price we pay for everything good in the world.

Whatever is good may be but the correction of something bad. Science is good because it overcomes disease, hunger, cold, distance, and drudgery. Companionship is good because it banishes loneliness. Education is good because it counteracts ignorance. If, as appears likely, every good is but some evil conquered, it follows that every evil is but a stepping-stone toward some blessing.

Teachers of religion love to dwell upon the arduous effort that commonly precedes high accomplishment. They are fond of discoursing upon the martyrdoms that advance cherished causes. Among their favorite topics are the sacrifices indispensable for achieving noble ends. Frequently they set forth how sorrow and difficulty can strengthen and purify character. The successful business man sometimes boasts that he got his education "in the university of hard knocks." We have also been reminded that whatever is bad, is bad because it conflicts with our ideals; the ideals themselves are good. All of this elucidates the constant interconnection of the good and the ill. We can hardly escape the conclusion that, where evil is not, good is not. Good and evil are part and parcel of the same reality. The only way to abolish evil is to abolish good, and the only way to abolish either would be to abolish the universe.

Such thoughts pertain, however, not so much to religion as to philosophy. Regarding the significance of the word "God," it suffices that there exists in the world not only trouble but also rescue from trouble. The word "God" becomes baffling not when people worship but when they argue; not when they experience, but when they deal with a report.

3. JUDAISM AND THE REPORTED

A superficial glance at Judaism leads one to suspect that, in Judaism, God is always something reported. In Jewish writings God is, again and again, represented as the world's Creator. The Bible, in its opening chapters, offers two distinct accounts of how the world was fashioned; and vestiges of other accounts lie scattered throughout the sacred collection. The Book of Psalms contains some splendid poems in which creation is the theme; while the Book of Proverbs, exuberantly lauding wisdom, pictures personified Wisdom as saying:

> The Lord made me as the beginning of His way . . .
> When He established the heavens, I was there . . .
> When He made firm the skies above . . .
> When He appointed the foundations of the earth
> (Proverbs 8.22, 26).

A poetic account of creation constitutes one of the most glorious chapters in the Book of Job (Chapter 38). During the Middle Ages, Jewish thinkers devoted much effort to combatting the Greek idea that the world had not been created but had existed from eternity; and, until recent decades, Rabbis have taken up the cudgels against scientific ideas that conflict with the traditional Jewish view.

Throughout the centuries, extraordinary Jewish ingenuity has been expended in the attempt to prove that the righteous are rewarded and the wicked punished, if not here and now, at least in the hereafter. Meanwhile, the doctrine that Israel is God's chosen, intimates that a supernatural power governs the destinies of nations. All of this appertains, of course, not to a God whom one experiences but to a God about whom one is apprised.

Pertinent here also is the atheism professed by some Jewish persons in our own generation. As already stated, the God denied by the atheist is a reported God. Experience is not subject to denial; only the reported is subject to denial. Those of us who find God in our experiences would encounter, both in Jewish tradition and in modern Jewish skepticism, much from which to dissent.

4. JUDAISM AND THE GOD OF EXPERIENCE

And yet, a more sustained look at Jewish teaching will disclose a different picture. We have noticed how frequently creation is celebrated in Jewish poetry. Poetry, indeed art of all kinds, is a

25

redemptive experience. A poem that truly stirs us delivers us from the depressing and the degrading. Those creation poems do not identify God with redemptive experience; but they place the name of God in the midst of such experience. Is not this already a step in the direction of equating God with that experience?

Again, how often in Jewish writings are the word "God" and the word "redemption" conjoined:

Return unto Me, for I have redeemed thee (Isaiah 44.22).

O Lord, my Rock and my Redeemer (Psalm 19.15).

With the Lord there is plenteous redemption (Psalm 130.7).

Blessed art Thou, O God, who hast redeemed Israel (Jewish Prayerbook).

Thou hast redeemed us from Egyptian bondage (Jewish Prayerbook).

Nor, when we have surveyed all the passages containing such words as "redeem," "redeemer," "redemption," have we exhausted the list. We must add such synonyms as "save," "deliver," "rescue," "deliverance," "salvation." God may be a reported God, but redemption is the chief thing reported concerning God. One need not go far beyond this in order to find God and redemption to be one and the same.

Capping it all is that group of Jewish outpourings in which experienced redemption is explicitly confessed as the meaning of the Divine:

I have no good but in Thee (Psalm 16.2).

In Thy presence is fulness of joy (Psalm 16.11).

The Lord is nigh unto the broken-hearted (Psalm 34.18).

As the stag panteth after the water-brooks,
So panteth my soul after Thee, O God.
My soul thirsteth for God, for the living God (Psalm 42.2, 3).

Only for God doth my soul wait in stillness (Psalm 62.2).

Whom have I in heaven but Thee?
And beside Thee I desire none upon earth.
My flesh and my heart faileth;
But God is the rock of my heart and my portion for ever . . .
But, as for me, the nearness of God is my good (Psalm 73.25, 26).

Happy is the one whose strength is in Thee (Psalm 84.6).

'The Lord is my portion,' saith my soul (Lamentations 3.24).

We might add the oft-quoted words of Judah Halevi: "I flee from Thee to Thee," or the stanzas in our hymn-book, translating that Hebrew hymn of the thirteenth century:

> Sweet hymns and songs will I recite
> To sing of Thee, by day and night,
> Of Thee, who art my soul's delight.

> How doth my soul within me yearn
> Beneath Thy shadow to return,
> Thy secret mysteries to learn!

> My meditation day and night,
> May it be pleasant in Thy sight,
> For Thou art all my soul's delight
> (Union Hymnal, No. 23).

The Hasidim, those flaming Jewish religious enthusiasts of Eastern Europe, cherish a poem whose tenor is:

> Where doth the Most High dwell?
> In the dwelling that admits Him.
> What is the dwelling that admits Him?
> 'Tis the dwelling clean and whole.
> What is the dwelling clean and whole?
> It is the lowly soul.

Obviously such language envisages the God of personal experience.

That seems also the import of the memorable passage in the Book of Hosea (2.22), "Thou shalt know the Lord" and a similar passage in the Book of Jeremiah (31.34), "They shall no more teach every man his neighbor, and every man his brother, saying: 'Know the Lord'; for they shall all know Me from the least of them unto the greatest of them, saith the Lord." Knowing the Lord is not the same as knowing *about* the Lord. These, and the frequent instances of the phrase "the knowledge of the Lord," contemplate, in all probability, not a God reported but a God whom we experience. That God, as an experience, is the focus of adoration in the Jewish prayerbooks and, above all, in the Jewish hymnbooks, can hardly have escaped our notice.

Then there is the Jewish conviction of God's omnipresence. The Psalmist exclaims:

> Whither shall I go from Thy spirit?
> Or whither shall I flee from Thy presence?
> If I ascend up into heaven, Thou art there;
> If I make my bed in the netherworld, behold,
>   Thou art there.
> If I take the wings of the morning,
> And dwell in the uttermost parts of the sea;
> Even there would Thy hand lead me,
> And Thy right hand hold me.
>   (Psalm 139. 7-10).

Not a few other examples of this discernment appear in the Jewish writings. One of the most arresting is the dictum of the Rabbis that the world does not contain God; God contains the world. If God is nowhere absent, God must indeed be a God whom we experience.

5. ANTHROPOMORPHISM

Another notable example lies in the Jewish aversion to anthropomorphism. Anthropomorphism means ascribing to God human qualities. The Bible and the Talmud abound in anthropomorphisms. Anthropomorphic are such phrases as "the eyes of the Lord," "the hand of the Lord," "the mouth of the Lord," "the

Lord heard," "the Lord spoke," "the wrath of the Lord." The Book of Daniel depicts how

> The thrones were placed,
> And one that was ancient of days did sit:
> His raiment was as white snow,
> And the hair of his head like pure wool (Daniel 7.9).

The Talmud, in a certain passage (Berakot 59A), pictures God as shedding tears over the misfortunes of Israel and, in another (Berakot 6A), as wearing phylacteries—the leather straps and cases such as the Orthodox Jew, while he recites the morning prayer, places around his left arm and around his brow. A notorious anti-Semite, Johann Eisenmenger, published, about the year 1700, a violent diatribe against the Jews in which, among other things, he vilifies the Jews because certain Hebrew books describe God in terms of physical immensity.

Notwithstanding this, the Jewish writings opposed to anthropomorphism have been noteworthy. Jewish literature speaks, ever so often, of God as "the Ineffable One." Does this not come near to saying the "non-reportable One"? Where the biblical text once read "to look upon the Lord," later editors changed the Hebrew vowels so as to make it read "to appear before the Lord." There was a time when Aramaic superseded Hebrew as the Jewish vernacular. In order to avoid anthropomorphism, a certain Aramaic translation of the Bible, instead of translating, often paraphrases. For instance, "The word of the Lord came unto me saying" is rendered "With me was the word of prophecy from before the Lord" (Ezekiel 21.13). "The mouth of the Lord of hosts hath spoken" becomes, in Aramaic, "Behold, through the word of the Lord of hosts, this hath been decreed" (Micah 4.4). Thus was anthropomorphism long ago mitigated by editors and by translators.

The outstanding opponent of anthropomorphism was the Jewish philosopher, Maimonides (1135-1204). Maimonides deemed it blasphemous to ascribe to God any attributes whatsoever. According to Maimonides, "God is good" should be interpreted not as imputing to God the attribute of goodness but merely as denying that God has attributes contrary to goodness. "God is one" should be understood to signify not that God possesses the attribute of unity but that God lacks the attribute of multiplicity. We can observe, even today, the contrast between the Christian readiness and the Jewish reluctance to endow the Deity with man-like traits. Negating an anthropomorphic God is, of course, virtually the same as negating a reported God. Deprive God of all attributes, and what is there reportable left over? When we meet God in our redemptive experiences, anthropomorphism no longer characterizes such expressions as "loving Heavenly Father," "The Lord is my shepherd" (Psalm 23.1), "Thy righteousness is like the high mountains" (Psalm 36.7), or "The Lord's hand is not shortened that it cannot save" (Isaiah 59.1). In the religion of experience, not a literal sense but a higher than literal sense attaches to these words.

To sum up: If, with the saints of all lands and ages, we use the word "God" to exalt and to vivify the redemptive aspects of experience, ours is a God beyond scientific challenge and immune to atheistic dispute. For the realization of that God, Judaism deserves no small measure of credit.

CHAPTER THREE

Righteousness

IF WE WOULD think clearly upon the subject of righteousness, our first step must consist in noticing how extensively conceptions of righteousness vary. We of this land and age pronounce slavery unrighteous; though millions in the past and many, no doubt, in some regions at present, would see in slavery nothing to oppose. We rate polygamy as unrighteous; but, in former centuries, perhaps even now in some parts of the world, polygamy would be countenanced and praised. There are those who deem it their duty to kill someone who belongs to a family some member of which may, at some time in the past, have slain a member of their own family. We call this the vendetta. To us, the vendetta is abominable. The staging of gladiatorial contests was, in ancient Rome, lauded and applauded, like bullfights in some countries today. But gladiatorial contests and bullfights strike those of our own culture as outrageous. Millions abhor, while other millions adore, Communism. The same may be said of lynching. Birth control is condemned by some and fervently advocated by others; likewise euthanasia, likewise military training, likewise protective tariff, likewise government aid to the unemployed and much else. The Orthodox Jew execrates praying with uncovered head; the opinion of the Reform Jew is the opposite. It can be asserted with little rashness that there is nothing right in human conduct anywhere but someone brands it as wrong and, conversely, there is no wrong deed anywhere but somebody, somewhere endorses or condones it.

These variations can occur in the life of one and the same individual. Every one of us today deplores having performed some act which, in bygone years, may have won his or her complete satisfaction. We can be sure that many of our doings which today seem commendable will, in years to come, overwhelm us with shame. And the converse may prove equally true.

In this matter, people are sometimes misled by language. It has been argued that there are some ethical judgments to which all people everywhere subscribe. Everyone agrees, for example, as to the unrighteousness of murder; and that is supposed to controvert what we have just said about ethical diversity. But such is not the case. It may well be that everybody who has ever lived has deprecated murder. Yet this implies no accord as to what it is that people designate as "murder." People antagonistic to capital punishment regard a death sentence as murder. Opponents of war view military action as murder. Meanwhile, mobs do not accuse themselves of murder when they lynch, nor do feudists rate feuding as murder, nor is dueling classed by duelists as murder. Emperor Nero surely did not name it "murder" when, "to make a Roman holiday," he had human beings devoured by lions; nor did the inquisitors label it "murder" when they burnt heretics at the stake. "Murder" is a word which people attach only to killings of which they disapprove. Something similar applies to theft, to adultery, indeed to any objectionable conduct. Correspondingly with "charity," "bravery," "honesty," or other terms of commendation; different people, different epochs, and different cultures exhibit different applications of those words. What one person calls "charity," another calls "pampering." The act that one person lauds as bravery is assailed by another as "recklessness" or "bravado." One person's "honesty" can be another's "tactlessness" or "fussiness" or "bad taste" or "indiscretion."

1. MUTUALISM AND RIVALISM

To find our way amid this welter, it will assist us if we mark out two broad divisions. Sometimes people are kind to one another, and sometimes cruel; sometimes they assist one another, and sometimes they fight; sometimes they detest, sometimes they love; sometimes they envy, sometimes they cooperate. Let us adopt the terms "mutualism" and "rivalism," mutualism referring to the various forms of concord, and rivalism to the several types of hostility. A mother's love for her child would exemplify the extreme of mutualism. War exhibits the extreme of rivalism.

That difference antedates human society. Naturalists have found both tendencies among animals and even among plants. To enlarge upon the rivalism in organic life, Charles Darwin coined such phrases as "natural selection," "struggle for existence," "survival of the fittest," and the poet Tennyson grieved at "nature red in tooth and claw." But other authors relate that the infra-human realms of nature display, in addition, trends toward kindliness. Such writers as Drummond, Kropotkin, Fiske, Nasmyth and, most recently, the Jewish writer, Ashley Montague, have pointed out that not only the life of human beings but also animal life and, in a way, plant life manifest not only depredation but also mutual aid.

The noted sociologist, Pitirim Sorokin, is at present engaged on a series of books reporting statistically the extent of loving-kindness in the affairs of mankind. However, we must not confuse the difference between mutualism and rivalism with the difference between right and wrong. All kinds of cruel acts have been commended and rewarded; and many a kind act has been reprobated and penalized. Aid and comfort to any human being is assuredly mutualistic. Yet, in wartime, we objurgate "aid and comfort to the enemy" as treason. In various of the occupied countries, during the second world war, it was criminal to shelter any Jewish man, woman, or child, mutualistic though such sheltering might have been. Meanwhile, the bombing of Tokyo and Hamburg was applauded by millions of Americans; and how some of us gloried in the devastation wrought by our atomic bomb! Punishment of all kinds is rivalistic; yet how many are willing to dispense with punishment in any form? Each human mind harbors enough rivalism to prompt the approval of many a rivalistic step and to stir displeasure at many a mutualistic step.

Those who read these words favor such mutualistic qualities as charitableness, faithfulness, politeness, companionability. Mutualism provokes our opposition when it takes the form of illicit love. Conceptions of illicitness vary from group to group. Among Catholics, love is reprobated if either of the parties has been previously divorced. In Italian countries and in Spanish countries, it is deemed improper for a young man to call upon a young woman or to "date" a young woman except under the strict chaperonage of some elder. Among Orthodox Jews, a man named Cohen—supposedly a descendant of the ancient Jewish priesthood—may not woo a widow or a divorcee. Among Jews of Eastern Europe, betrothal is forbidden if the woman's first name is the same as that of the man's mother or if the man's first name is the same as that of the woman's father. Intermarriage between a Jewish person and a non-Jewish person still awakens remonstrance even among Jews of a liberal stripe. Though we may not share the prepossessions of the Catholics or of the South Europeans or of the East European Jews, all of us would undoubtedly oppose polygamy or promiscuity, despite the mutualism that infuses every love relationship.

Still, it is possible for mutualism to operate even here. Rigid propriety in one's own sexual behavior can be combined with understanding and compassion for others. Welfare work for the sexually erring is commonly undertaken by persons who are themselves beyond reproach. The sexually conforming are also the people least disposed to feel rancor toward those who, as liberals, would widen the scope of the sexually permissible. Prudes and fanatics are, ever so often, people who have strayed in their own sexual conduct.

Mutualism and the doctrine of ethical relativity are singularly connected. All intolerance grows out of the persuasion that one's own conception of right and wrong is the only conception worth respecting. All strife, all bigotry, all persecution, all warfare proceed from that assumption. Men will never cease destroying one another as long as the notion prevails that there is an absolute right and an absolute wrong, always identical, of course, with one's own conception of right and wrong. All religions, non-Jewish as well as Jewish, veer away from mutualism and in the direction of rivalism when they regard their own appraisals as supreme and other appraisals as beneath consideration.

2. JUDAISM AND RIVALISM

Let us now explore how Judaism can vivify our ethical thinking. Rivalistic urges obtain vigorous expression in many reaches of Jewish literature. This, as might be expected, develops most markedly in connection with war. We might quote, as a sample, a passage from that war song, the eighteenth Psalm (verses 39, 43) :

> I have smitten them through, so that they are
> not able to rise . . .
> Then did I beat them small as the dust before
> the wind;
> I did cast them out as the mire of the streets.

Another resounding example is furnished by the Song of Deborah in the fifth chapter of the Book of Judges, a song said by scholars to constitute the oldest piece of Hebrew literature extant. The Song of Deborah describes a war between the Hebrews and Canaanites in which the Hebrews, though outnumbered and not well-equipped, won an overwhelming victory. The woman, Deborah, was the Hebrew leader. The poem narrates, among other things, how the Canaanite leader, Sisera, fled from the battlefield and sought refuge in the tent of Heber, a nomad. None was in the tent at the time except Jael, Heber's wife. According to one account, while Sisera slept; according to another, while his view was obstructed by a large bowl from which the famished warrior drank milk that Jael had fetched for him; Jael took a hatchet and dashed out his brains. Such is the theme of Deborah, a theme savage and ferocious. How

Deborah gloats over Sisera's braining! With what glee she recounts the heartbreak of Sisera's mother waiting, in vain, for her son's return! We have here rivalism unmitigated.

Penalties of death, scourging, or excommunication are imposed by the Bible and by the Talmud not only for murder, kidnapping, rape, or false testimony but also for working on the Sabbath, for "witchcraft," for adultery, for heresy, even for youthful excesses of eating and drinking. God Himself is sometimes portrayed as exterminating hosts of people for the derelictions of some ruler or leader. Many of us are familiar with the passage in the Second Commandment in which the Lord threatens to visit the iniquities of the fathers upon the children, the grandchildren, and the great-grandchildren. This comports with the ancient principle of corporate responsibility, that is, punishing an entire family or an entire city, or an entire nation for the misdeeds of one or a few of its individuals.

A rivalistic bent is also reflected in the Talmudic attitude toward the uneducated. Unkindly remarks are leveled at the ignoramus— in Hebrew, the *Am Ha-Aretz*, the "rustic." That seamy side of learning, disdain for the unlearned, is not absent from the Rabbinic pages.

3. JUDAISM AND MUTUALISM

These rivalistic strains, however, serve but to render the more impressive the counterbalancing mutualism:

Thou shalt not oppress thy neighbor or rob him (Leviticus 19.13).

Thou shalt not go up and down as a talebearer among thy people (*Ibid.*, 19.16).

Thou shalt not hate thy brother in thy heart (*Ibid.*, 19.17).

Thou shalt not take vengeance, nor bear any grudge . . . but thou shalt love thy neighbor as thyself (*Ibid.*, 19.18).

And if a stranger sojourn with thee in your land, ye shall not do him wrong . . . and thou shalt love him as thyself (*Ibid.*, 33, 34).

These are the things that ye shall do: Speak ye every man the truth with his neighbor; execute the judgment of truth and peace in your gates; and let none of you devise evil in your hearts against his neighbor; and love no false oath (Zechariah 8.16, 17).

What is hateful unto thee, do not unto another (Sabbath 31A).

The greatest of heroes is he who changeth a foe into a friend (Abot de Rabbi Nathan 23.1).

Better to be persecuted than to be a persecutor (Baba Kama 93A).

Be gentle and yielding as a reed, not hard and proud as a cedar (Ta'anit 20A).

Judge not thy fellow man until thou standest in his place (Abot II, 5).

Distinctly mutualistic is the Jewish concern for the poor and the oppressed:

When ye reap the harvest of your land, thou shalt not wholly reap the corner of thy field, neither shalt thou gather the gleaning of thy harvest. And thou shalt not glean thy vineyard; thou shalt leave them for the poor and for the stranger (Leviticus 19.9, 10).

If there be among you a needy man, one of thy brethren . . . thou shalt not harden thy heart, nor shut thy hand from thy needy brother (Deuteronomy 15.7).

Happy is he that considereth the poor (Psalm 41.2).

He that is gracious unto the poor lendeth unto the Lord (Proverbs 19.17).

Those are passages from the Bible. The Talmud asserts that benevolence is tantamount to all other meritorious deeds combined (Baba Batra 9A). Akin to this is the Jewish compunction about charging interest:

If thy brother be waxen poor, and his means fail with thee, then shalt thou uphold him . . . Take no interest of him or increase . . .

Thou shalt not give him thy money upon interest, nor give him thy victuals for increase (Leviticus 25.35-37).

The Rabbis of a later age maintained that "charging interest is tantamount to committing all the sins in the world" (Exodus Rabba 31.13).

To these may be added the prophetic protests against "turning aside the way of the poor," "despoiling the poor," "selling the poor for silver and the needy for a pair of shoes," "grinding the faces of the poor." Allied also are the laws against taking, as a pledge, a millstone or the garment of a widow; or against obtaining a pledge by entering a poor person's house instead of remaining outside for the pledge to be brought by the pledger; also the requirement that a pledged garment be returned to the pledger every evening, for the garment which a poor person wore by day had to serve also as his bedcover by night. The twenty-fourth chapter of the Book of Job reads almost like a modern pamphlet inveighing against social ills:

> The poor of the land must hide . . .
> They go forth to their labor;
> They must hunt the desert for sustenance,
> There is no harvest for the homeless.
> They must harvest fields that are not theirs . . .
> Naked must they pass the night for lack of clothes,
> They have no covering from the cold.
> They are drenched by the downpour of the mountains,
> They must embrace the bare rock for want of shelter.
> They must go naked without garments,
> Hungry they must carry the sheaves.
> Shut in by walls, they must press the oil;
> Thirsty, they must tread the wine press.

Particularly humane are the arrangements for the considerate treatment and manumission of slaves. Nor is the Rabbinic disdain of the ignoramus, the "rustic," untempered. The duty of aiding the ignorant to surmount their ignorance is frequently and force-fully urged. A singularly fine passage likens Israel to a vine:

The householders are the branches,
The scholars are the clusters,
The "rustics" are the leaves.
The clusters should pray for the leaves
Because, without the leaves, the clusters could not be (Hullin 92A).

Another passage maintains that the learned often originate in "rustic" homes (Sanhedrin 96A). The Talmud is not at all content with intellectual snobbery.

4. JUDAISM AND UNIVERSALISM

While the Bible harbors many warlike utterances and sentiments, it also preserves some of the grandest declarations of the peace ideal to be found anywhere:

He shall judge between nations,
And shall decide for many peoples;
And they shall beat their swords into plowshares,
And their spears into pruning-hooks;
Nation shall not lift up sword against nation,
Neither shall they learn war any more
                    (Isaiah 2.4; Micah 4.3).

He maketh wars to cease unto the ends of the earth;
He breaketh the bow and cutteth the spear in sunder;
He burneth the chariots in fire (Psalm 46.10).

Even more peace-minded is the Talmud. The Talmud singles out virtually every one of the military leaders mentioned in the Bible and pictures him not as a fighter but as a scholar, not as a warrior but as a man of books. Says the Talmud: "God found for Israel no surer vehicle of blessing than peace" (Ukzin III.2).

We have alluded to the war poem known as the Song of Deborah. The Rabbis of a later age gave an interpretation which

turns that fury into its very opposite. The Song of Deborah ends
with the words:

> So perish all Thine enemies, O Lord;
> But they that love Him be as the sun
> When he goeth forth in his might (Judges 5.31).

As many as three times, the Talmud quotes the saying:

> They who are reviled but revile not others, they who hear them-
> selves reproached but make no reply, they whose every act is one
> of love and who cheerfully bear their afflictions, these are the
> ones of whom Scripture saith: 'They that love Him be as the
> sun when he goeth forth in his might' (Yoma 23A; Sabbath 88B;
> Gittin 36B).

How ingeniously the Rabbis transmute utmost rivalism into utmost
mutualism!

The Bible tells about the wars between the Hebrews and the
Moabites. But the Bible also includes the Book of Ruth in which
Ruth, the Moabite daughter-in-law, speaks to Naomi, the Judean
mother-in-law, words of devotion that have never been surpassed:

> Entreat me not to leave thee,
> And to return from following after thee;
> For whither thou goest, I will go;
> And where thou lodgest, I will lodge;
> Thy people shall be my people,
> And thy God my God . . .
> The Lord do so unto me, and more also,
> If aught but death part thee and me (Ruth 1.16).

The Bible records the deadly conflicts between the Hebrews
and the Assyrians. The Assyrians destroyed the Northern Hebrew
Kingdom, and subjugated and all but destroyed the Southern
Hebrew Kingdom. Notwithstanding this, the Bible canonizes the
Book of Jonah which narrates how Jonah, the Hebrew prophet,
is divinely constrained to warn the city of Nineveh concerning its
sins, thus winning Nineveh to repentance and to God's forgiveness.

Nineveh, be it remembered, was the capital of Assyria, Israel's relentless foe.

Egypt, also one of Israel's oppressors, was at the same time the dread rival of Assyria. Yet one of the prophetic books predicts:

> In that day shall there be a highway out of Egypt to Assyria, and the Assyrian shall come into Egypt, and the Egyptian into Assyria; and the Egyptians shall worship with the Assyrians. In that day shall Israel be a third with Egypt and Assyria, a blessing in the midst of the earth; for that the Lord of hosts hath blessed him, saying: 'Blessed be Egypt My people, and Assyria the work of My hands, and Israel Mine inheritance' (Isaiah 19.24).

In later ages, when the doctrine of a life hereafter had gained headway in Judaism, a noted Rabbi averred that the righteous of all nations shall have a portion in the world to come (Tosefta Sanhedrin 13.2).

5. THE ROLE OF MERCY

While the Jewish writings have much to say about punishment, they also dwell extensively upon forgiveness. The Day of Atonement, which was originally a day for certain occult purification rituals in the sanctuary, became later a day of divine and human pardon. And that is the day which, down to our own generation, holds the foremost place in the Jewish religious calendar. When the Book of Proverbs (16.6) declares, "By mercy and truth iniquity is expiated," it voices a conception of atonement which can not be transcended.

The doctrine of corporate responsibility was abandoned far back in the centuries. Both the prophet Jeremiah (31.29) and the prophet Ezekiel (18.2, 3) protest against the maxim:

> The fathers have eaten sour grapes,
> And the children's teeth are set on edge.

The Hebrew Law itself, in the Book of Deuteronomy (24.16), explicitly prescribes:

The fathers shall not be put to death for the children, neither shall the children be put to death for the fathers;

and the Second Book of Kings (14.6) states specifically that King Amaziah observed that law when, punishing the assassins of his father, "the children of the murderers he put not to death."

The severe biblical penalties for adultery and for juvenile delinquency are so interpreted by the Rabbis of a later age as to effect their virtual abrogation. The Rabbis (Baba Kama 83B) similarly explained away: "Eye for an eye, tooth for a tooth" (Exodus 21.24). We ourselves might question whether that maxim, in the first place, meant anything more than a figurative way of saying that punishment should be just and not excessive. Capital punishment was practically discontinued under Rabbinic jurisdiction.

While Jewish teaching does not achieve the extreme mutualism of abolishing punishment altogether, it goes far in that direction when it diminishes the role of punishment as a factor in human controls. Not only is the doctrine of corporate responsibility completely abandoned, and not only are various penalties reduced or relegated to the hereafter; but, over and above this, the thought occurs repeatedly that the good is to be practiced for its own sake, not from hope of reward or from fear of retribution. One of the renowned sages taught: "Be not like those who serve for pay, but be like those who serve without expecting pay" (Abot I.3).

Something of like tenor may, on occasion, reside in the doctrine that, for many a wrongdoing, the punisher is God. Leaving punishment in the hands of God can, at times, amount to withdrawing it altogether from the hands of men. This also illustrates Jewish mutualism.

6. PEACE OF MIND

Rabbi Joshua Loth Liebman, whose untimely death was mourned by vast numbers, was the author of that immensely popular book, *Peace of Mind*. Here and there, in ancient Jewish writings, one finds Hebrew equivalents of "peace of mind." A certain verse in the Book of Isaiah (26.3) is commonly, though incorrectly, translated: "Thou wilt keep him in perfect peace whose mind is stayed on Thee." The Rabbinic books frequently extol "serenity of spirit." But the Jewish outlook exhibits a still closer approach.

Our peace of mind depends upon our relationship with other human beings. By and large, that relationship is one of competition. Competition prevails not only in business and industry; it extends through all human pursuits. People compete with one another for influence and prestige. Lawyers and physicians compete with one another not only for clients and for patients but also for ranking and eminence in their professions. College professors compete with one another for the attachment of their students as well as for renown in scholarship and authorship. Actors and orators compete with one another for the applause of their audiences. Young people compete with one another for the attentions of the opposite sex. Students compete with one another for academic and athletic prizes. Everyone craves to be accounted better looking than someone else, or better circumstanced or better housed or better attired or better educated or more important than someone else. The scope of competitiveness knows hardly a limit.

It is this competitiveness that generates much of our mental turmoil. To outstrip others requires unceasing vigilance and exertion. Even that does not always suffice. While our attention is fixed on one competitor, we are outdistanced by another. Once outrivaled, we are racked with envy. What we suffer from envy probably exceeds what we suffer from any other one cause.

But sometimes our competitiveness undergoes a lull. Now and then we step out of competitiveness into cooperativeness. Exalted moments enter our lives when we seek no longer to outstrip, outshine, and outrival others but strive instead to help others and promote the interests of others and are willing, for the sake of others, ourselves to be obscured. Then it is that we attain peace of mind. The essence of mental peace is non-competitiveness.

While the ancient Hebrew language contains no word for non-competitiveness, it has a word which means the same as non-competitiveness. That word is: *humility*. In Jewish teaching, pride is ever deprecated and humility ever extolled:

Unto Him will I (God) look,
Even on him that is poor and of a contrite spirit (Isaiah 66.2).

It hath been told thee, O man, what is good,
And what the Lord doth require of thee:
Only to do justly, and to love mercy, and to
walk humbly with thy God (Micah 6.8).

The Lord is nigh unto them that are of a broken heart,
And saveth such as are of a contrite spirit (Psalm 34.19).

The sacrifices of God are a broken spirit;
A broken and a contrite heart, O God, Thou wilt
not despise (Psalm 51.19).

With the humble is wisdom (Proverbs 11.2).

Such are utterances from the Bible. Rabbinic literature proffers thoughts like these:

Before them that revile me, may my soul keep silent and may my soul be as the dust before all (Berakot 17A).

God ignored all other hills and mountains and caused His presence to rest on Mount Sinai—Sinai of little height. He ignored all goodly trees and made His presence rest on the thorn-bush (Sotah 5A).

Of the haughty spirited, God saith: 'I and he can not dwell in the same world' (Sotah 5A).

Humility is the greatest of all excellences (Abodah Zarah 20B).

Said Hillel: 'My lowliness is my exaltation, my haughtiness is my degradation (Exodus Rabba 45.5; Leviticus Rabba 1, 5).

And humility brings peace of mind. Not inadvertently is the verse from the hundred-and-thirty-first Psalm,

> Lord, my heart is not haughty, nor
>   mine eyes lofty;
> Neither do I exercise myself in
>   things too great, or in things too
>   wonderful for me,

followed by the verse,

> Surely I have stilled and quieted my soul;
> Like a weaned child with his mother.

Humility, non-competitiveness, peace of mind—how they all belong together! And how, in this nexus, mutualism reaches its acme!

7. OUR OWN CHOICE

To us of today, the mutualistic strains in Judaism will surely appeal. What Judaism upholds regarding charity, social justice, world peace, perhaps even what it urges regarding humility, will captivate our souls. Our problem of problems will stem from our personal shortcomings, as a passage in the Talmud clearly discerns. A Jewish saint of Talmudic times would pray thrice daily:

> Lord of all worlds, it is known unto Thee that we yearn to do Thy will. What prevents our doing Thy will? The leaven in the dough (Berakot 17A).

"The leaven in the dough" is figurative for the inclination to act contrary to our ideals. How that Talmudic outburst differs from expressions, both ancient and modern, which treat sin as if it were susceptible of swift or sudden correction! Change of character takes place neither instantly nor rapidly. For the overcoming of certain of our flaws, there may be needed months or years of discipline, training, and experience. Various of our defects may even prove incurable, as that Talmudic supplication intimates. Our only recourse is to be aware of our plight. We can avoid blindness. When our conduct violates our ideals, we can be conscious of that violation. We need not be obtuse to the discrepancy between what

we should be and what we are. We can concur in the words of
the Psalmist who beseeches:

>Search Thou me, O God, and know my heart,
>Try me and know my thoughts;
>And see if there be any way in me that is grievous,
>And lead me in the way everlasting (Psalm 139. 23, 24).

Every expectation of forgiveness, repentance, or regeneration must
be prefaced by that insight.

CHAPTER FOUR

Judaism

THE FACT THAT we are subject to the label "Jewish" poses one of our momentous problems. We often hear it asked: "How is the word 'Jew' to be defined?" The difficulty with this question grows out of an erroneous assumption, an assumption which we have already pondered (page 16), the assumption that every word bears only one meaning. Most words show a variety of meanings. We recalled how Webster's Unabridged Dictionary offers 18 definitions of "watch," 14 of "star," 18 of "carriage," 36 of "head," and 41 of "run." There are 44 definitions of "point."

1. THE MANY JEWISH TYPES

A Jew can be a person who adheres to the customs of the Old World; a Jew can also be one who follows American ways entirely. A Jew can be someone steeped in Hebrew lore; a Jew can also be utterly ignorant of Hebrew and uninterested in Hebrew. A Jew can be a person who, though a citizen of the United States, regards himself as belonging, in some sense, to the State of Israel. A Jew can also be an American who vigorously resents such imputation. A Jew can be someone who credits, as actual occurrences, the miracles described in the Bible and in the Talmud. A Jew can also be someone who repudiates not only the belief in miracles but likewise all the other synagogal teachings. A Jew can be one who, three times a day, recites certain Hebrew prayers. But there are myriads of Jewish people who have never heard of those prayers, and hosts of Jewish people who detest praying of all kinds. There are millions of Jews who, like the martyrs in the time of Antiochus

Epiphanes, would sooner be tortured to death than eat the flesh of a swine. Meanwhile, all of us know Jewish persons who, without compunction, include pork products in their diet. For millions of Jews, Saturday is like any work-day; but there are other millions who shrink in horror from such Sabbath desecration as answering a telephone or turning on or off an electric light, before sundown Saturday and after sundown Friday.

Most Jewish persons would find it incomprehensible how anyone can be called a Jew if he worships Jesus. Yet, nineteen and a half centuries ago, when the worship of Jesus began, it started in a Jewish environment. Only after the worship of Jesus was adopted by populations with whom the Jews were in conflict, did the Jewish worshipers of Jesus disappear. Some of the few Jewish individuals who have, in our own time, become converted to Christianity call themselves "Hebrew-Christians"—purporting, in this way, to represent a revival of that original Jewish-Christian sect. Such converted Jews are regarded by Jewish people of all other classifications as entirely outside of the Jewish fold, despite the fact that those converts cling to many of the old Jewish beliefs such as the belief in the supernatural and infallible character of the Bible. By contrast, Jewish persons not of that group rank as reputable and even honored members of the Jewish community, though they may have rejected most or all of those ancient doctrines.

There are Jews who are Negroes, such as the Falashas of Ethiopia and, in New York City, several congregations of Jewish colored people with a ritual and an organization uniquely their own. We have also heard of Chinese Jews and of Hindustani Jews, the Beni-Israel, as well as of Mexican Indian Jews.

2. ORTHODOX, CONSERVATIVE, REFORM

The customary classification of Jews into Orthodox, Conservative, and Reform does not, by any means, cover all of these diversities. To understand those divisions, we must view them not as separate compartments but as vaguely located positions on a yardstick. We would place, at one end of our stick, Orthodoxy in its extreme form. We have alluded to the Orthodox Jewish scruples about the Sabbath, about daily prayers, and about certain articles of diet. But the scope of Orthodox rigidity is much vaster. An illustration would be the requirement that the brother of a married man who dies childless must wed the deceased man's widow. Inasmuch as the laws against polygamy might render such marriage impossible, there must be performed a curious old ritual of shoe-removing by which the widow exempts her brother-in-law from that obligation. Orthodoxy prohibits the wearing of garments made of cloth containing both wool and linen; a garment must be completely the one or the other. It is forbidden to eat the fruit of a tree sooner than the fifth year of its fruit-bearing. Orthodoxy imposes not only the fast of Atonement Day but many fasts in addition, such as the fast of the Ninth of Ab, associated with the destruction of the Temple at Jerusalem, or that of the Seventeenth of Tammuz, connected with the first breaching of the wall of Jerusalem by the Romans, or the fast of the Tenth of Tebeth, the date on which the final siege was started by the Babylonians. There is also a Fast of Gedaliah, the day after the Jewish New Year, mourning the assassination of a certain ancient Jewish governor; and likewise the Fast of Esther, the day before Purim, because Esther is reported to have fasted before appealing to King Ahasuerus. Some Orthodox Jews fast also on the last day of every month—"the minor Day of Atonement," as it is called. Some fast every Monday and every Thursday, the days on which, in addition to Saturday, the scroll is publicly read in the synagogue. Orthodoxy prescribes many prayers of which not even vestiges remain in the prayer books of Reform. We need hardly mention the strict rule that, on all ritual occasions, the head must be covered; although scholars inform us that, until the sixteenth century or later, the covering of the head was optional. These are only a few samples of usages no longer remembered in our own Jewish group, yet scrupulously heeded by Jewish persons near the Orthodox end of our yardstick.

Orthodox Judaism also entails a copious system of beliefs. Such men as Maimonides (1135-1204), Joseph Albo (1380-1444), and Simon Duran (1361-1444) undertook to formulate the doctrines which Jews were supposed or required to hold. These doctrines included the belief that God created the world out of nothing; that, at Mount Sinai, God revealed Himself to Israel and conferred the Jewish law; that everything stated in the Bible is true beyond all question; that God rewards the upright and punishes the wicked either here or hereafter or both; that God alone and none else is to be worshiped; that, in due time, God will restore Israel to a former state of autonomy, prosperity, and happiness by sending the Messiah. "Messiah" means "the Anointed One," in allusion to the inaugural anointing of the ancient Hebrew kings.

We have placed, at one end of our yardstick, the Jewish persons who observe all of the rituals and accept all of the tenets. At the other end are those who observe none of the rituals and reject all of the tenets or have never heard of those rituals or tenets. Between these two extremes, stand Jews of all gradations, Jews retaining some of the rituals but not others, favoring some of the doctrines but not others. The portion near the one end we have called Orthodoxy, the portion somewhat short of the other end we call Reform, and that which lies between the two we call Conservatism.

Even within these segments, we descry broad variations. Among Orthodox Jews, some are less Orthodox and some are more Orthodox. Some Reform Jews have abandoned more of the old beliefs and customs and some not quite so many. Some Conservative Jews approximate Orthodoxy, and some approximate Reform. Some Conservative congregations have so far approached Reform as to allow a few prayers in English, and confirmation services in which girls participate as well as boys, and the seating of men and women on the same floor of the synagogue, even if in separate sections of the same floor; in Orthodox synagogues, the women occupy the gallery. Those Conservative congregations, at the same time, heed such Orthodox requirements as the covering of the head, the wearing of the prayer-shawl, the observance of two days for every holiday except the Day of Atonement, and the reading of the scroll without the abridgment preferred in our Reform Temples.

Not a few Conservative Jews and even Orthodox Jews, especially among the educated, while punctiliously following many of the old ceremonials, have abandoned most of the old beliefs, such as the belief in miracles, in supernatural reward and punishment, and in the colorful and romantic Jewish past pictured in the Bible and in the Talmud. Jews tend to slough off the old doctrines long before discontinuing the old observances.

3. THE WORD "JEW"

The word "Jew" originated not in early Biblical times but in later Biblical times. It will be recalled that, after the death of King Solomon, about 931 B.C.E., the Hebrew nation split into two parts, the Northern part seceding from the Southern. The Northern Hebrew Kingdom was overthrown by the Assyrians in 722 B.C.E. The Southern Hebrew Kingdom survived 136 years longer. It was then destroyed by the Babylonians.

The Northern Hebrew Kingdom disappeared completely. Its survivors, carried off as captives to Assyria, amalgamated with their conquerors. We refer to that obliterated Northern Kingdom when we speak of "the lost ten tribes." With the Southern Hebrew Kingdom, it was otherwise. Those additional 136 years made a tremendous difference. The influence of the prophets is credited with the fact that, though the Babylonians deported the ablest people of the Southern Kingdom, especially its promising youth, that Southern Hebrew group never lost its identity. The Babylonian deportees took with them the written or remembered words of the great prophets, Amos, Hosea, Isaiah, Micah, and Jeremiah. They retained their religion, though they lost their nationality.

The Southern Kingdom which continued for those additional 136 years consisted of the tribe of Judah and the tribe of Benjamin.

Soon the latter became absorbed in the former. The result was that, not long after the year 722 B.C.E., the tribe of Judah was the only surviving member of the Hebrew confederation. "Hebrew" (or "Israelite") and "Judean" became synonymous. An English contraction of "Judean" is "Jew." It is inaccurate to state that the "Jews" escaped from Egypt or that the "Jews" received a revelation at Mount Sinai or that the "Jews" worshiped the golden calf or that the "Jews" took David as their king. It were like saying that Christopher Columbus discovered the United States of America. The periods at which those Biblical events occurred or are supposed to have occurred antedated the time when "Judean" and "Hebrew" (or "Israelite") became co-extensive.

Once the word "Judean" grew current, it gathered a number of new meanings. First the word denoted a certain nationality. Then it signified the religion nurtured in that nationality. Then it implied that religion detached from the nationality; people of other nationalities could become Jews by adopting the cult. Later the word designated not only adherents of that cult but also the descendants of those adherents, even after the descendants had altered or discarded the ancestral beliefs and practices. Whether we are Jews by religion or by nationality has become, in our own generation, a matter of raging controversy. History shows the word "Jew" attached sometimes to either, sometimes to both, and sometimes to neither—as happens when a person is "Jewish" for no other reason than that of having had Jewish parents or grandparents.

The meanings of the terms "Jew," "Jewish," "Judaism" are further complicated by the fact that those words serve not merely to name. Those words have the additional force of divulging the user's feelings. This is the import of the word "Jewish" when Orthodox Jewish people insist that whoever works on Saturday is a Jew no longer or that whoever denies the Biblical miracles is a Jew no longer. By contrast, the Talmud maintains: "Once a Jew always a Jew, sin as he may" (Sanhedrin 44A).

Jewish persons ordinarily employ the word "Jew," "Jewish," "Judaism" in a commendatory sense. They speak of "Jewish learning," "Jewish charity," "Jewish ideals." Among anti-Semites, the connotation is the opposite. The anti-Semitic use is always deprecatory. Anti-Semites speak of "Jewish knavery," "Jewish trickery," "Jewish treachery." Hitler uttered the words "Jew," "Jewish," "Judaism" only in scorn. Never did he attach those words to anything which did not evoke his detestation.

4. MISLEADING PHRASES

This background should put us on our guard against certain phrases current in our midst. These phrases are:

A. The Chosen People
B. The Mission of Israel
C. The Preservation of Judaism
D. Jewish Unity

A. It hardly needs telling that "Chosen People" betrays anthropomorphism. A chosen people implies a God who does the choosing. Such a God is distinctly manlike and not at all in accord with that aversion to anthropomorphism which has marked much of Jewish thinking. We might, of course, avoid the anthropomorphism by taking the words in a higher than literal sense. We could construe the phrase as a reference to some gleaming aspect of Jewish history. Yet it is hard to see how Jewish history warrants such an estimate. Jewish influence upon the world has resembled the influence of any other people upon the world; that influence has emanated not from the masses but from the few. In a higher than literal sense, there have been chosen individuals like Jeremiah, Johanan ben Zakkai, Maimonides, Spinoza, Bergson, Einstein. "Chosen" can be predicated of geniuses, not of the rank and file.

B. Similarly anthropomorphic is "Mission of Israel," unless we think of a mission not as something supernaturally imposed but as something which the individual himself elects. But, here again, it is not the masses, whether of Jews or Christians or Mohammedans or Americans or Italians, that institute the great projects. It is the gifted handful. Certain exceptional individuals in every cult or nation may be credited with a mission. For any group *en masse*, it is difficult to understand how "mission" can be the appropriate word.

C. "Preservation of Judaism" invites a number of questions. Since Judaism embraces so many types, which is the type whose preservation we shall seek? And just why this type and not another? Again we might ask: In an always changing world, how can we know the shape of the future? How can we be sure which of today's views or practices will, in ages to come, prove or not prove worthy of retention?

To understand the phrase "preservation of Judaism," we must notice the context in which it appears. The phrase is almost invariably employed by those who advocate some specific step or program. "We must build a finer Temple so that Judaism might be preserved," "We must organize a Hebrew class so that Judaism might be preserved," "One must marry a Jewish person, because it is only through that kind of marriage that Judaism is preserved," "We must support the State of Israel, that Judaism might be preserved," "We must start a Jewish youth society, so that Judaism might be preserved," "We must kindle lights on Friday evening, we must refrain from work on Saturday, we must worship with covered heads, so that Judaism might be preserved."

Be it noticed, in each of the above sentences, the important part is not the second part but the first part. The first part is clear and unequivocal. The second part is not. The second part illustrates rationalization. In psychology, rationalization is the term which pivots on the distinction between our professed reasons and our true reasons. The reasons which people advance by way of argument are rarely, if ever, the reasons by which they are actually impelled. Arguments usually proclaim motives calculated to make a favorable impression, not the motives that really operate. According to some psychologists, our real motives are unconscious motives, hidden from our own selves and buried in the depths of our minds and susceptible of detection only by an intricate technique of psychoanalysis. What people really want is not some hazy "preservation of Judaism," but a new Temple, a Hebrew class, a youth society, abstinence from intermarriage, the State of Israel, candle-lighting, head-covering, or some other ritual conformity. Their genuine reason may lie concealed from themselves as well as from us. "Preservation of Judaism" is their rationalization.

D. Finally, how shall we understand the appeals for "Jewish Unity"? So varied are the people who carry the label "Jewish," that lack of unity should not astonish us. What should astonish us is the extent to which cooperation does take place among those different factions.

Jewish unity reaches its maximum in Jewish benevolences. While Jews and non-Jews cooperate extensively in works of social welfare, separate Jewish agencies continue in several fields, partly because of tradition, partly because of subtle factors which sometimes make understanding between Jews and Jews easier than understanding between Jews and non-Jews, and partly because of the need for division of labor. The realm of charity is so vast that it has seemed best for separate groups to serve separate clienteles.

In the United Jewish Appeal, there is participation by Jewish persons of all kinds. Recently some dissatisfaction with the United Jewish Appeal was voiced by the American Council for Judaism. The objection pertained, however, not to the benevolences of the United Jewish Appeal but to its allocation of certain funds for Zionistic propaganda. Jewish persons of all descriptions are supporters of the National Jewish Hospital at Denver, of the Leo N. Levi Memorial Hospital at Hot Springs, and of the Hebrew Sheltering and Immigrant Aid Society which counsels and assists newly arrived Jewish immigrants. The several Jewish regional orphan asylums and homefinding societies, as well as the many local Jewish family service bureaus and Jewish hospitals, draw support from Jewish persons of all classifications.

If benevolence is the sphere of maximum unity, worship is that of maximum separateness. Here the differences are pronounced and irreconcilable. Considering how widely Jewish persons vary as to their countries of origin and as to their educational and economic background, how can it be otherwise? We sometimes hear of mergers or proposed mergers between Reform congregations and Conservative congregations. The wisdom of such mergers might well be doubted. Is it not better for people to live apart as friends than to live yoked together quarreling?

The degree of unity achieved by Jewish educational programs somewhat exceeds that achieved by Jewish worship. Still greater is the degree of cooperation in recreational projects for Jewish children and youth, although the cooperation exhibited by these recreational projects falls short of that exhibited by Jewish benevolence. Many persons with meager attachment to tradition find fault with Jewish centers for their recourse to certain nationalistic and ritualistic symbols, while the dearth of such symbols displeases Jewish persons at the other extreme.

5. OUR OWN DECISION

Amid all of this multiplicity, what shall be our own attitude?

How we shall think, is not for others to dictate. Ours is the more arduous assignment. Each must decide for himself and for herself what direction to take.

The following is possible: We can center our lives in the ideal of spirituality. Spirituality means that non-competitive attitude toward others and that reverence for human personality which we have already considered (pages 19, 20). Aspects of spirituality are patience, self-forgetfulness, helpfulness, affection, good will. These we can exalt as paramount. Other people may accord dominance to rituals or to Jewish nationalism or to the study of Hebrew and of

Jewish history. Still others may emphasize Jewish distinctiveness, stressing as all-important anything that differentiates Jew from non-Jew. With our own position, none of these would coincide. This does not imply that, for those who differ, we shall feel contempt; such contempt would violate the spiritual ideal. Spirituality need not even involve the exclusion of those other interests from our lives. It does entail that, if we retain any of those other attachments, their place in our lives shall be secondary. The spiritual shall be primary.

These spiritual values can constitute our Judaism—Judaism in the appreciative import of the term. Those values can be Jewish in the meaning of "Jewish" not when the word labels but when it commends, Jewish in the sense in which everything good and noble is "Jewish."

This does not gainsay that spirituality is Jewish also in the other sense of the term. The great Jewish books embody spiritual commitments in language of unrivaled power and beauty. Yet the inception of that outlook in the Jewish past need not be our reason for adopting it today. We would extol that outlook even if it had not been thus propounded. We would take issue with the Jewish teachers, we would espouse those values even if they had been disparaged by the Jewish teachers. We choose the spiritual values not because of any ancient recommendation. We elect them because they grip our souls. We embrace them because, through them, we experience God.

Meanwhile, the fact deserves emphasis that most of us are Jewish by birth. That brings us into frequent contact with others of like designation. Jewish are perhaps most of our friendships. Our associates in many of our undertakings are Jewish. Our marital choice is likely to be Jewish. These Jewish relationships exist. Let it be our concern to make them blessed.

We can be conscientious about our Jewish benevolences. In our day, a great deal of benevolence has become non-sectarian or inter-sectarian. To the Community Chests we shall refer later (page 88). Most of the money expended for social welfare in the United States is money raised by taxation, completely obliterating the distinction between Jews and non-Jews both among the givers and among the recipients. Forward-looking Jewish persons have expressed the view that, in some areas in which the distinction still operates—for example, the domain of community centers—mergers might prove advantageous, particularly in the smaller cities. Since 1848 there has existed, in Greater New York, the Community Service Society which serves both Jewish and non-Jewish clients in the boroughs of Manhattan, Bronx, and Queens. On the Board of this Society, and in its various lay advisory committees, sit Jewish persons as well as non-Jewish persons. Jewish persons as well as non-Jewish persons are on its staff and in its contributing public. Meanwhile, areas remain in which the demarcations still prevail—perpetuated, to some extent perhaps, by the need for a division of labor; the Catholics to do what they can for the Catholic needy, the Protestants for the Protestant needy, and the Jewish group for the Jewish needy; while all jointly should succor those who fall outside of these rubrics. Spirituality would place benevolence high among the priorities of our budget.

Our Jewish connection may also induce us to investigate various forms of Jewish worship. Some of these forms might appeal. Some of them might be so modified as to make them appeal. Or we might, in conjunction with our Jewish friends, create new forms of Jewish worship. This is, in fact, already being done, particularly by some groups of Jewish youth. We should by no means overlook the possibility of using our Jewish associations to further our spiritual upreach.

Whatever we do, we can cling to the spiritual. We can let the spiritual and naught else stand first. Would not that be a fruitful way of defining our Judaism?

CHAPTER FIVE

Prayer

THE PRAYERS that are printed in books are by no means the only prayers that people offer. Countless are the prayers that arise spontaneously in the human heart.

1. THE VALUE OF PRAYER

Does prayer do any good? To treat this question, we must first dispose of another question, namely: Are prayers ever answered? Are petitions to God ever granted? Are prayers efficacious?

Against the efficacy of prayer, it is easy to argue. One can readily observe that, if prayers were efficacious, nobody would ever get sick or die or succumb to trouble; all that would be needed would be to beseech God for protection. It could be pointed out that the belief in the efficacy of prayer contradicts the belief in God's goodness. A God who, in response to prayer, sends help would be a God who, in default of prayer, withholds help. A father who lets his children perish simply because, for some reason or other, there was no appeal for deliverance, is hardly the God of those who favor the offering of prayer. One can recall instance upon instance in which prayers, though many and fervent, have proved futile. One need only mention the world's chronic state of war, despite billions of prayers for peace; or the world's persistent wickedness, despite ages of praying for the kingdom of righteousness. There are, to be sure, numerous stories telling how prayers have come true. But these stories can be countered by the many cases in which realization never occurred. There is enough good in the world for happy turns of events to arrive occasionally after the prayers for such turns of events, and to arrive soon enough thereafter to create the illusion of fulfilment.

All of this we can concede. And yet none of this really invalidates prayer. Despite anything that can be said against prayer, prayer can be precious.

A. Prayer can articulate our ideals. People pray for those things that they most intensely desire. That is why people pray for recovery from illness, for rescue from want, and for escape from trouble. That is also why some people pray for purity of heart, for faithfulness to duty, and for calm in the face of adversity. Prayer puts ideals into words.

B. For the things that they crave, people strive. Prayer can be a part of that striving, an incident in that striving, especially when the objects of one's striving are the graces of character.

C. Prayer can be a form of literary art. Some of the prayers in the Bible and in the Talmud and in the old prayer books, and not a few of the prayers composed in modern times, even some spontaneous prayers, are literary masterpieces, with extraordinary power to purify, to elevate, and to inspire.

D. Behind every prayer, stands that by which the prayer is prompted. Prayers can be prompted by hatred, like the war-time prayers for the annihilation of the enemy. Prayers can also be prompted by sordid ambition, like prayers for the winning of a prize-fight or a ball game or an election. Often prayers exemplify nothing better than dull mechanical routine, motivated by nothing higher than to do as others do or by some superstitious assumption that praying might bring good luck.

But prayers need not be of those descriptions. Prayers can be the outpourings of love and aspiration. The finest of our prayers are those which we offer sincerely in behalf of others. Such prayers arise from deep and earnest affection. "He prayeth best who loveth best," said the poet Coleridge. Every day, millions of prayers confirm the poet's words.

These attributes imbue prayer with a highly redemptive value, and that means divine value. To those for whom the word "God" signifies love and idealism, prayer can be literally a communing with the Most High. Love and idealism are the loftiest form of redemption, and God means redemption; and in prayer, love and idealism reach their grandest verbal expression. Even prayer for something material can embody a spiritual import. Prayer can relate our material wants to our spiritual goals.

Regarding the second person of the pronoun in prayer, a noted sociologist has reminded us that, in the use of the second person, prayer is not unique. It is in the second person that most of our thinking proceeds. Do we not always, in our thoughts, imagine ourselves expounding our thought to someone else? In prayer we use the pronouns "Thou," "Thy," "Thine," "Thee." "Do Thou, O Lord, sustain me," "Thy mercy is everlasting," "Thine is the greatness and the glory," "Unto Thee do I lift up my soul." But does not thinking of all kinds show much the same trend? We may not, in our ordinary thoughts, use the sacred singular of the pronoun. Yet, almost invariably when we think, we carry in our minds the image—even if but a dim and vague image—of someone to whom we phantasy ourselves addressing our ideas. If you will pause and mentally formulate some plan or some argument, you will notice how, all but inevitably, you imagine someone to whom your plan or argument is being communicated. Prayer is an impressive instance of the same tendency.

2. PRAYER IN JUDAISM

Virtually everything that we have said concerning prayer finds illustration in Judaism. The belief in the efficacy of prayer has won extensive Jewish acceptance. In the Bible, Isaac efficaciously entreats God that his wife Rebecca might become a mother. Miriam, because her brother Moses prays for her, recovers from leprosy. In answer to his prayer, the lost strength of the blinded Samson is restored long enough for him to pull down the pillars of the Philistine temple, thus killing the three thousand Philistines assembled to jubilate over his plight. King Hezekiah prays and thereby gets well from a desperate illness. The Talmud and the Jewish historian Josephus tell about a noted saint named Onias whose prayers, especially prayers for rain, invariably brought results. The Talmud acquaints us with Hanina ben Dosa, capable, we are told, of prayers which would induce God to heal the sick. In Eastern Europe, there have long existed the Hasidim, an enthusiastic sect of Jewish mystics, whose Rabbis allegedly achieve marvels by means of prayer. The entire Jewish prayer book rests upon the assumption that its prayers will tend to bring about the health, the wisdom, the well-being, and the political freedom which are the ends which those prayers envisage.

Still, as regards the efficacy of prayer, the Jewish writings are not without their misgivings. The Psalmist complains, with unqualified candor:

> O my God, I call by day, but Thou answerest not;
> And at night, and there is no surcease for me (Psalm 22.3).

If people like Onias and Hanina ben Dosa or, in more recent times, the Rabbis of the Hasidim can utter prayers of amazing efficacy, the implication obtains that, from the prayers of others, this efficacy is lacking. Hanina ben Dosa himself admitted that his prayers were not always fruitful. When people continue praying despite their doubts about the efficacy of prayer, does that not prove that factors other than efficacy underlie the practice?

3. IDEALISM IN JEWISH PRAYER

Of the Jewish sayings on the subject of prayer, one of the noblest is this:

> If one prays that the needs of another be fulfilled, those same needs will first be fulfilled in the life of the one who does the praying (Baba Kama 92A).

How obviously this applies when the needs in question are the needs of the spirit!

Of no little impressiveness, from our standpoint, are those prayers in the Bible which are not monologues but dialogues; prayers in which, when man speaks to God, God speaks in return to man—God, in fact, taking the initiative. When God and Adam converse about the forbidden fruit, it is the voice of God that begins the interview. Abraham entreats God in behalf of the wicked city of Sodom, but not until God himself broaches the problem. In the dream of the heavenly staircase with the angels descending and ascending, God speaks to Jacob; Jacob speaks only after he awakens. At the burning thornbush, God first announces His presence, then Moses responds. The child Samuel supplicates: "Speak, Lord, for Thy servant heareth"—but not until the Lord has called thrice. Similarly when Isaiah, looking upward from the sanctuary, beholds the heavenly seraphim or when Jeremiah, contemplating the almond tree, perceives the resemblance between the Hebrew word for "almond" and the Hebrew word for "watchful," it is God's utterance that opens the discourse. The same characterizes several of the Psalms. One of the prophetic books quotes God as actually promising: "I will answer *before* they call" (Isaiah 65.24).

Whether those narratives are history or myth is beside the point. Those accounts may be legendary. The fact remains, nevertheless, that the writers of those accounts and the repeaters of those accounts did endorse a momentous conception of prayer. With them, prayer is not always a monologue. It can be a conversation with God, and a conversation which God originates. One might almost say that man does not pray to God until God first prays to man. And how that conception appeals! The most significant aspect of prayer may reside in that by which the prayer is preceded. The love, the idealism, the aspiration by which the prayer is impelled—herein may lie the prayer's supreme meaning. Our own prayers can thus also be conversations with God, God being present in the exaltedness of spirit by which the prayer is motivated.

Of prayer as an articulation of ideals, Jewish writings afford abundant illustration:

> O send out Thy light and Thy truth; let them lead me
> (Psalm 43.5).

> Thou desirest truth in the inward parts (Psalm 51.8).

> Create in me a clean heart, O God, and renew a steadfast spirit within me (Psalm 51.12).

> Before my revilers may my soul keep silent, and may my soul be as the dust before all (Berakot 17A).

> Purify our hearts that they may serve Thee in truth
> (Jewish Prayer Book).

> O favor us with knowledge, understanding, and discernment!
> (Jewish Prayer Book).

There is a Talmudic passage in which God is represented as praying to Himself. The prayer of God to God reads thus:

> May it be My will
> That My compassion vanquish My wrath,
> That My compassion prevail over My other attributes,
> That I treat My children according .
> To My attribute of compassion,
> And deal with them not according
> To the strict letter of the Law (Berakot 7A).

The content of that prayer can intrigue us, even though we may be loath to subscribe to that conception of the Divine.

4. SUPERSEDED IDEALS

The ideals embodied in some of the Jewish prayers are such as we of today no longer endorse. This applies to certain prayers growing out of various ancient wars and suffused with the bitterness which characterizes wars wherever waged, our own wars of today being no exception. An example would be that supplication in the Book of Psalms (79.6):

Pour out Thy wrath upon the nations that know Thee not.

Then there is the hymn of hate in Psalm 109:

Let his days be few . . .
Let his children be fatherless,
And his wife a widow.
Let his children be vagabonds, and beg;
And let them seek their bread out of their
    desolate places,
Let the creditor distrain all that he hath;
And let strangers make spoil of his labor.
Let there be none to extend kindness to him;
Neither let there be any to be gracious to
    his fatherless children.

Jewish scholars assert that this prayer, though appearing in the Book of Psalms, is not Jewish. They contend that those hateful words constitute not a prayer offered by the Psalmist but a prayer quoted by the Psalmist as the words of his enemy, to illustrate the imprecations that he suffers from his enemy.

Also among well known Jewish prayers are those imploring the restoration of the Jewish state:

Lift up the ensign to gather our exiles,
And gather us from the four corners of the earth . . .
Restore our judges as at first
And to Jerusalem, thy city, return in mercy . . .
And to Jerusalem, Thy city, return in mercy . . .
Rebuild it soon in our days as an everlasting building,
And speedily set up therein the throne of David
                    (Jewish Prayer Book).

Many of us no longer cherish that ideal. The only nation to which we regard ourselves attached is the United States. Persons who frequent the services in our American Reform Temples may have grown familiar with the prayer which reads:

> Fervently we invoke Thy blessing upon our country and our nation. Guard them, O God, from calamity and injury; suffer not their adversaries to triumph over them, but let the glories of a just, righteous and God-fearing people increase from age to age. Enlighten with Thy wisdom and sustain with Thy power those whom the people have set in authority, the President, his counselors and advisers, the judges, law-givers and executives, and all who are entrusted with our safety and with the guardianship of our rights and our liberties. May peace and good-will obtain among all the inhabitants of our land; may religion spread its blessings among us and exalt our nation in righteousness. Amen (Union Prayer Book).

Ancient Jewish teachers stress praying in the synagogue or at least in a quorum of ten. The Jewish prayer book nonetheless supplies prayers for private use. Our most earnest praying is likely to be that which issues from our souls when we are alone, as the Bible presents Jacob at Beth-El, Moses at the burning thorn-bush, and Amos, Isaiah, and Jeremiah, each at the moment of his Divine summons.

The Bible speaks of those who, when praying, kneel like Solomon or Ezra or who prostrate themselves like Abraham or Joshua. Those who prostrate themselves in prayer are mentioned with respect also by the Talmud. To this day, worshipers fall upon their faces in Orthodox synagogues at certain moments on the High Holy Days. For all that, some Jewish persons rabidly oppose kneeling. The reason lies in their impression (albeit erroneous impression) that kneeling is peculiarly Christian. Our own attitude should be that the matter of importance is not the worshiper's posture but the worshiper's motivation. With rare aptness, the Talmud remarks: "Eyes down, heart up—that is the way of prayer" (Yebamot 105B).

5. SPONTANEOUS PRAYERS

The Jewish teachers of old imposed no requirement that prayers be recited in Hebrew. That ancient Jewish law code, the Mishnah, maintains: "Any language is suited to prayer" (Sotah VII, 1). Kindred are the thoughts of a Jewish preacher, Elijah ben Solomon Abraham, who lived in Smyrna, Turkey, some two hundred and fifty years ago. The following are some of his reflections:

> God considers not the literary forms of the supplication but its fervor (Me'il Zedakah, 346).

> Though one may not know the proper way of reciting a prayer, God does, nonetheless, grant one's supplication (*Ibid.*, 669).

> Certain verses in the Book of Psalms mean: Hearken unto my prayer, though it consist only in the stretching forth of my hand, my heart being dead within me from affliction and incapable of thought (*Ibid.*, 946).

> One may be mentally confused, and yet one's prayer can count with God as if it duly set forth one's needs (*Ibid.*, 949).

> God will listen to the mere sound of a cry which, though unformed into a supplication, issues from a troubled person's mouth (*Ibid.*, 1468).

> Provided the intent be worthy, God's lovingkindness will enfold any man or woman who, because of the Hebrew, may fail to understand the prayer and commit mistakes in the reciting (*Ibid.*, 1667).

Whether we agree or disagree with Elijah ben Solomon Abraham, we cannot but recognize the compassion and the altruism—in our own terminology, the mutualism—investing the author's soul and animating his words.

While certain fixed prayers may have been prescribed under the old Jewish system, spontaneous prayers are by no means discouraged. The Talmud names two noted teachers who, discussing the objectionableness of praying that is mechanical and perfunctory

(Abot II, 18), define such praying as that in which the worshiper fails to insert anything in his own words (Berakot 29B). Rabbinic writings contain some splendid prayers which were composed without any ritual intentions. Some examples are these:

> Lord of all worlds, redeem, deliver, save, and rescue us from pestilence, war, and plunder; from blight and mildew, and from all calamities to which the world is subject. Thou who wilt answer ere we call—blessed art Thou, O Lord, Restrainer of the plague (Ketubot 8B).

> May it be Thy will, O Lord, our God, that there may dwell among us love and brotherhood, peace and friendship. Enlarge Thou our boundaries spiritually. Prosper us with a future hope. Place Thou our portion in Paradise. Keep us aright through good associations and good inclinations. May we awaken in the morning to find our heart's hope in the revering of Thy name and our soul's serenity in Thy blessed presence (Berakot 16B).

A famed Rabbi of the third Christian century proposed, as a morning prayer: "I thank Thee, O Lord, my God, that Thou hast brought me out of darkness into light"; as an afternoon prayer: "May it be Thy will, O Eternal, my God, that as Thou hast vouchsafed my seeing the sun at its rising, Thou also vouchsafe my seeing it at its setting"; and as an evening prayer: "May it be Thy will, O Eternal, my God, to bring me out of darkness into light" (Genesis Rabba 68.11). These prayers, illustrating deviations from the ritual, illustrate at the same time literary charm. They also illustrate idealism, particularly if we take the references to darkness and to light in a figurative sense.

6. REVERENCE AND MODERATION

We of today raise no issue whatsoever with the Jewish books when they urge that praying be coupled with reverence. Says the Mishnah, that ancient law code: "People should pray only when in a devout mood" (Berakot V.1). Later teachers expanded this into the admonition:

People should not pray when in a state of distraction, indolence, flippancy, small talk, levity, or petty concerns. Prayer should exemplify the joy of performing a sacred act (Berakot 31A).

Another passage in the Talmud declares:

> Whoso prayeth audibly is a person of little faith;
> Whoso prayeth loudly is one of the false prophets
> (Berakot 24B).

Rabbi Meir, one of the greatest of all Jewish sages, once stated that the decisive thing in prayer is not the sound of the voice but the intent of the heart (Megillah 20A). We of today subscribe to these convictions. Our persuasion, however, should take the form of heeding these compunctions in our own practice. They should not take the form of censuring the people who deviate.

The Talmud also cautions against excess. Certain extremists of old are said to have devoted to prayer nine hours of every day. They followed the rule of reciting the liturgy every morning, every afternoon, and every evening. Over each recitation, they would tarry an hour. Before each recitation, they would spend a preparatory hour of rest, and after each recitation, a supplementary hour of meditation (Berakot 32B). The practice did not meet with unqualified approval. The ancient teachers realized that such inordinate piety might result in neglect of study and in remissness at occupations. From that criticism, no modern person is likely to dissent.

Jewish tradition has regarded prayer both as a privilege and as a duty. We of today do not regard prayer as a duty. We would be at a loss for reasons to support any claim that prayer is obligatory. Prayer must be completely optional to possess value. We must pray because we long to pray and not for any other reason. The prayer for which our hearts yearn—that and only that is the prayer that can inspire and that can burgeon out of motives which are exalted and therefore divine.

CHAPTER SIX

Social Idealism

SOCIAL IDEALISM marks religion of the advanced and modernistic kind. It characterizes the new-fashioned in religion rather than the old-fashioned. While social idealism prevails extensively in the Bible and considerably in the Talmud and the Midrash, official Judaism has, throughout the ages, tended to stress rituals, and official Christianity to stress theology. Traditional religion supports personal ethics rather than social ethics. Questions such as those of wages and working hours, collective bargaining, full employment, race relations, housing, child labor, civil liberties, family limitation, immigration, and the like have, on the whole, remained secular. It was in the latter part of the nineteenth century that socially minded people, both among Christians and among Jews, began to religionize social ideals.

1. SOCIAL ACTION

In the year 1885, a group of Reform Rabbis held a conference in Pittsburgh and adopted a series of resolutions defining the position of Reform Judaism on such subjects as ceremonials, authority, mission of Israel, holiness, the hereafter, Palestine, and other points of theology. These pronouncements occupied seven paragraphs. Then, on the initiative of Emil G. Hirsch, a young man destined to become the leading Rabbi of his generation, the Pittsburgh Conference added paragraph eight. This paragraph reads:

We deem it our duty to participate in the great task of modern times, to solve, on the basis of justice and righteousness, the problems presented by the contrasts and evils of the present organization of society.

This was the first of a long series of pronouncements emanating not only from organizations of Jews but also from those of Catholics and Protestants. Year by year, since that time, resolutions of a social tenor have been produced by the various denominations. A worthy sample of such pronouncements was the platform adopted by the Central Conference of American Rabbis in 1918. As that platform reads, it calls for:

1. A more equitable distribution of the profits of industry.

2. A minimum wage which will insure for all workers a fair standard of living.

3. The legal enactment of an eight-hour day as a maximum for all industrial workers.

4. A compulsory one-day-of-rest-in-seven for all workers.

5. Regulation of industrial conditions to give all workers a safe and sanitary working environment, with special reference to the needs of women.

6. Abolition of child labor and raising the standard of age wherever the legal age-limit is lower than is consistent with moral and physical health.

7. Adequate workmen's compensation for industrial accidents and occupational diseases.

8. Legislative provision for universal workmen's health insurance and careful study of social insurance methods for meeting the contingencies of unemployment and old age.

9. An adequate, permanent national system of public employment bureaus to make possible the proper distribution of the labor forces of America.

10. Recognition of the right of labor to organize and to bargain collectively.

11. The application of the principles of mediation, conciliation and arbitration to industrial disputes.

12. Proper housing for working-people, secured through government regulation where necessary.

13. The preservation and integrity of the home by a system of mothers' pensions.

14. Constructive care of dependents, defectives and criminals with the aim of restoring them to a normal life wherever possible.

Later a clause was added inviting friendliness toward immigrants and steps toward their Americanization.

In 1928, the Central Conference of American Rabbis again formulated a platform, this time introducing such proposals as the prevention of lynching, the conservation of civil liberties, and opposition to military training in schools and colleges. In 1930, a paragraph was appended recognizing the desirability of birth control for the sick and the impoverished. Later years brought resolutions beseeching justice for the exploited share-croppers, urging a federal Fair Employment Practices Act, calling for the constructive use of atomic energy, and favoring American aid for the economic development of backward countries—President Truman's "Point Four." Similar proposals have been advanced from time to time, by other Jewish bodies such as the Rabbinical Assembly of America (a Conservative Rabbinic organization), the National Council of Jewish Women, and the National Federation of Temple Sisterhoods. Kindred ideals, with variations, of course, corresponding to the differences among the several sects, also imbue pronouncements of Catholics, Presbyterians, Baptists, Methodists, Lutherans, Quakers, Ethical Culturists, Unitarians, and Universalists, indeed of nearly all denominations. In 1932, there was established the National Religion and Labor Foundation in which representatives of organized labor meet with priests, pastors, and Rabbis for the purpose of exploring the interests they have in common and of determining the possibilities of cooperation.

Nor has social vision been limited to discussions and resolutions. In many instances, the different religious bodies have combined for practical action. The Central Conference of American Rabbis, the

Federal Council of Churches (now called the National Council of Churches), and the National Catholic Welfare Council have together aided striking miners and have studied the disaffections of workers in a hosiery mill. They have jointly investigated the lockout which once occurred on the Western Maryland Railroad. These same three bodies have collaborated in conferences on unemployment and on consumers' cooperatives and in issuing appeals against slums and against infringements upon civil liberties.

In scores of cases, Rabbis have served as industrial arbitrators.

Now, social vision is more pronounced on the national level than on the local level. The themes of labor relations, housing, civil liberties, military training, race relations, and the like are not so frequently subjects of pulpit discourse as they are topics of debate and action at national conferences. Such stalwarts as Emil G. Hirsch, Stephen S. Wise, Edward L. Israel, among the Jews, and Bishop Brent, Bishop Fowler, Father Ryan, John Haynes Holmes, Harry Emerson Fosdick, Washington Gladden, and Cardinal Mundelein, among the Christians, have given social justice a conspicuous position in their preaching. Numerous other Rabbis, pastors, and priests have, from time to time, handled these themes. Nevertheless, the problems with which preaching has more commonly dealt have been personal rather than social. This may be due to the fact that most people are more concerned about the personal than about the social. It may also be due to the fact that social issues are likely to be controversial issues. To espouse a controversial position in the pulpit is, as a rule, unfeasible. During a religious service, the dissenter in the pew is not free to answer back. Most Temples and churches hold gatherings outside of the religious services, gatherings such as forums, panels, debates, and lectures followed by questions and answers. At assemblies such as these held, as a rule, not in the sanctuary but in a church or Temple annex, social questions can be argued most advantageously, for the simple reason that there can be a hearing of both sides.

2. EFFECTIVENESS OF SOCIAL ACTION

The question has often been raised whether, with their social pronouncements, religious bodies ever do any good. Do those clerical and Rabbinic declarations ever influence current practice or legislation? Does anyone, except the few conference delegates who vote on the social justice resolutions, ever pay any attention to those resolutions?

Whatever conclusion one may reach on this point, one fact stands out: Virtually every one of the social welfare measures instituted by the states or by the nation has been advocated by some religious group or groups, years and sometimes decades earlier. One of the great eras of social legislation in the United States was that of the New Deal inaugurated by President Franklin D. Roosevelt in 1933. The New Deal introduced federal initiative or participation in old age security, aid for dependent children, insurance against unemployment, insurance of bank deposits, subventioned housing for the lowest income groups, slum clearance, and labor exchanges. Add to these: legal provision for a minimum wage, for limitation of industrial working hours, and for the adjustment of industrial conflicts; abolition of child labor; and the legally assured right of workers to organize for collective bargaining. These have been adopted long ago. Federal health insurance, while not yet adopted, has been under consideration. Yet, every one of these had, long before its enactment, been urged by various religious groups both Jewish and Christian. Turn back to page 71 and notice how almost every item in the social justice platform of 1918 prognosticates developments of nearly two decades later. And various of those measures had been proposed both by Jewish groups and Christian groups long prior to 1918.

Even if we question whether religious pronouncements have been effective, we need not deny that religious action may have been the straw indicating the direction of the wind. Legislative measures await a favorable public opinion. Religious action can be a sign of public opinion. Religious action may not have been the cause of the governmental action; but both the governmental action and the religious action may have been effects of the same underlying cause. That underlying cause was the trend of the times.

Not a few people feel persuaded that, in at least one instance, religious action was decisive. This occurred in connection with the twelve-hour day and seven-day week which prevailed once in the manufacture of steel. Those inordinately long hours had become a national scandal. The situation became so disturbing that President Harding assembled the steel manufacturers at the White House and besought them to alter that shocking schedule of hours. The steel operators responded that they would submit the question to the Iron and Steel Institute, a body of experts consulted by the industry regarding the processes and arrangements for steel production. The Iron and Steel Institute duly rendered its decision, which was that the twelve-hour day and seven-day week was entirely proper and practical and that neither workers nor employers would benefit by the change. That seemed to settle the question in favor of the prevailing way. But there was a young Rabbi in Rochester, New York, the late Rabbi Horace J. Wolf. Rabbi Wolf was, at the time, chairman of the Commission on Social Justice in the Central Conference of American Rabbis. Rabbi Wolf, though far from being an expert on the production of steel, dared question the experts' opinion. Rabbi Wolf invited the Protestant body, the Federal Council of Churches, as well as the National Catholic Welfare Council, to join the Central Conference of American Rabbis in a nationally declared protest against the twelve-hour day and seven-day week. The Protestants and the Catholics responded without hesitation. A joint protest was published June 5, 1923. On July 6, 1923, exactly one month later, the chairman of the United States Steel Corporation announced that the twelve-hour day and the seven-day week was to be discontinued. It appears that, where the President of the United States had failed, religious action succeeded—and succeeded in the face of opposition by the Iron and Steel Institute, whatever the influence of that body may have been.

3. RELIGION AND SOCIAL IDEALISM LINKED

How do these endeavors come to be linked with religion? Attempts to religionize social concerns appeared ages ago. The prophets in the Bible arraigned those who exploited the poor. A striking example is the passage from Amos:

> Hear this, O ye that would swallow the needy,
> And destroy the poor of the land,
> Saying: 'When will the new moon be gone,
>   that we may sell grain?
> And the sabbath, that we may set forth corn?'
> Making the measure small, and the price great . . .
> 'That we may buy the poor for silver,
> And the needy for a pair of shoes' (Amos 8.4, 5).

Similar are the utterances of Isaiah:

> The Lord will enter into judgment
> With the elders of His people, and the princes thereof:
> 'It is ye that have eaten up the vineyard;
> The spoil of the poor is in your houses;
> What mean ye that ye crush my people,
> And grind the face of the poor?' . . . (Isaiah 3.14, 15).

> Woe unto them that join house to house,
> That lay field to field,
> Till there be no room, and ye be made
>   to dwell alone in the midst of the land! (Isaiah 5.8).

As we noted on pages 37, 38, mitigating the lot of the poor and the defenseless occupies a notable part of Biblical legislation. The Talmudic compunction about fairness to the laborer and the Midrashic antipathy to the charging of interest (also broached on page 38) have much in common with the modern advocacy of collective bargaining and of social security. An example of Talmudic scruple about the rights of manual workers is furnished by passages such as these:

> An employer may not compel his workers to begin work earlier in the day or to stop work later in the day than is the custom in that locality (not even for a higher wage). He must provide them their meals and due seasoning for their food, if such be the local custom (Baba Mezia VII. 1).

> Rabbi Johanan ben Matya once directed his son to go and hire some laborers. The young man, carrying out that request, entered into some stipulation with the laborers regarding their meals. When the son reported this to the father, the father remarked: "My son, hadst thou feasted those laborers like Solomon in all his glory, thou wouldst not have exceeded thy duty. Are they not sons of Abraham, Isaac, and Jacob?" (*Ibid.*).

Such social idealism as exists in the synagogues and the churches of today may well have derived encouragement from those ancient patterns.

This, of course, is by no means the same as saying that those ancient writings wield authority. If social purpose is commendable, it is commendable no matter what the ancient writings assert one way or the other. If social purpose is undesirable, nothing in those writings can make it otherwise. Even for those who call the sacred writings "authority," those writings exert no authority. Regardless of their opinions about the holy books, all people are selective. People select, from the holy books, those views to which they subscribe, and ignore or overlook or misinterpret those to which they do not subscribe. Some people emphasize the social vision in those books. Yet throughout the ages and in many quarters to this day, stress is laid not on the social contents but on the ritual or theological contents. Some people prefer one set of contents, some prefer another; and this occurs among Christians as well as among Jews. The final authority is the individual soul. Emerson spoke wisely when he said: "The soul is the measure of all things."

While the social vision of the ancient writers may form a linkage between religion and social purpose, it is not the chief linkage. A profounder linkage derives from the religionizing of mutualism. We have treated mutualism in Chapter III. An obvious type of mutualism is compassion. Compassion is religionized when mutualism is religionized; and compassion for the underprivileged generates a social outlook.

Social effort can also emanate from rivalism. Social endeavor can be prompted not only by love for the poor but also by hatred for the rich. Social purpose not rarely employs acrimonious language. Invectives against "plutocrats," "capitalists," "big business," and "the ruling classes"—not to mention "union bosses"—abound in this field.

Whether mutualism shall prevail or rivalism shall prevail is a matter of individual choice. This much only can be urged: let us recognize the difference. Let us not get the two confused. If we choose mutualism, let us term it mutualism or some equivalent. If we choose rivalism, let us term it rivalism or some equivalent.

4. THE IMPLICATIONS OF MUTUALISM

Mutualism would call for singleness of purpose. We can profess devotion to the cause of labor and yet be actuated not by devotion to the interests of the working people but by animosity toward employers and financiers. Under the guise of helping the underprivileged, we can vent our envies or our prejudices against the privileged.

There is such a thing as our Ego. Ego—the Latin for the first person pronoun, "I"—is a word which we apply to the fact that we are elated when someone praises us and dejected when someone adversely criticizes us. There are certain opinions which we hold so intently that those opinions and we become identified. Our Ego gets bound up with those opinions. We are contented when those opinions are endorsed, and nettled or vindictive when those opinions are defied. The opinions themselves may be valid and worthy, and yet the discussion of those opinions can so implicate our Ego as to make it not our opinions but our Ego that will command our exertion. Mutualism would require sharp caution on this point.

When in a controversial mood, we often ignore our opponent's personality. We hold our opponent in contempt. It does not occur to us that our opponent may be as sincere as we are. We do not realize that the urge constraining our opponent to think as he does is as irresistible as the corresponding urge in ourselves. If mutualism is to be our ideal, this violates our ideal.

To our opponent, our views are mentally upsetting. Do we regret our opponent's mental upset? We often enjoy his upset. Is this mutualism? This applies whether we are liberal or conservative, radical or reactionary.

We impute to our opponent sinister motives. He imputes to us sinister motives. We know our opponent's imputations to be remote from the truth. May not our own imputations be similarly remote from the truth? If there is anything that eludes our knowledge, it is other people's motives. Psychologists apprise us that even our own motives lie beyond our ken.

The climax of unwisdom is reached when we and those opposing us engage in argument. Here is where, to use a phrase from the Book of Job, we "darken counsel with words." Arguments between protagonists of opposing views never convert either side. The effect is but to strengthen each side in its prepossessions. Such arguing accomplishes nothing except disturbed emotions and excess of talk. Meanwhile, the more logical one's reasoning, the more one's opponent is humiliated and mortified. Mutualism does not willingly humiliate or mortify anyone. As we would ourselves be spared humiliation and mortification, so are we, if mutualistically inclined, unwilling to humiliate or mortify someone else; particularly since humiliation and mortification, intensifying our antagonist's resentment, only increases his passion in behalf of the opposing side.

The role of argument is that of winning those whose minds are not yet made up. For those who are already committed, argument is useless. When people are open-minded, we can tell them our doctrine. If we inform them truthfully and interestingly, we serve those people and serve our cause. This is far different from wrangling with someone who is already convinced to the contrary.

5. A REVISED VIEW OF COURAGE

These controversies entail, among other things, misleading conceptions of courage. We constantly hear courage lauded. No other theme figures more frequently in sermons, lectures, and ethical writings. People overlook the consideration that there is nothing good about courage in itself. All depends upon the purpose which the courage is to serve. A bandit is courageous; but who applauds a bandit except another bandit? It takes courage to be an assassin. Where anti-Semitism encounters opposition, as it does in some parts of the world, it requires courage to be an anti-Semite. Our soldiers are courageous; but the soldiers of the enemy are likewise courageous. In the days of the conflict over slavery, Elijah Lovejoy, the Alton, Illinois, printer was a paragon of courage. Because of his anti-slavery agitation, Lovejoy lost his life. Of course, people in that day extolled courage; but they execrated Lovejoy in the very next breath.

Courage, even when it is good, is an evil symptom. When conditions are as we would have them, courage is unnecessary. It takes courage to rush into a burning house in order to save a human life; but how much better it would have been had the conflagration never occurred! It calls for courage to rescue someone from drowning; but how much more satisfying it would have been had the precautions at the waterfront been ampler! William Lloyd Garrison evinced remarkable courage when he advocated the abolition of slavery. How much more desirable it would have been had the slavery or the ruffianism never existed! David, facing Goliath, was exceedingly brave; but how much happier it would have been had the Hebrews and the Philistines contrived to have no war at all but to live side by side in peace!

Wherever there is human conflict, both sides are in peril. And the conflicts roused by social issues rage bitterly. On both sides courage becomes indispensable and inevitable. For all that, as we have said, there is something weightier than intrepidity. All-essential is the purpose which the courage promotes. We should look well to the goals of courage before we acclaim courage. If the goal be ostentation and retaliation, there is nothing to praise. If the goal, with reasonable prospects of attainment, be the relief of human suffering, then indeed is courage admirable. Too often is courage the excuse for inconsiderateness and indiscretion. The highest courage may, at times, consist in risking the charge of cowardice.

Better than encomiums on courage might be the aim of so ordering human society that the need for courage might diminish. Intelligence rather than bravery, insight rather than daring, helpfulness rather than boldness might prove the more fruitful course. The evils of society might be treated not as a battle to be fought but as a problem to be solved. Who knows but that progress may be awaiting precisely that attitude!

6. THE COMPLEXITY OF THE PROBLEM

The pursuit of social justice offers wide scope for applying the adage about practicing what we preach. While we condemn the avaricious employer, it might be well for us to inquire whether we ourselves as employers or employees are fair and humane. While we inveigh against greedy landlords, let us make sure that we are clean of greed ourselves. Before we clamor for freedom of speech, let us be solicitous that we ourselves grant freedom of speech and refrain from putting in jeopardy those who advocate the views that we combat. Assuming that our religion is a religion of mutualism, those assuredly are points at which religion and social idealism merge.

No doubt the readers of this book favor good housing for all; civil liberties, race equality, and comfortable livelihood for all;

social security, educational opportunities, and adequate health care for all. It is wise and proper to join organizations which seek to promote these ends, to contribute to the finances of such organizations and, so far as time and strength permit, to participate in their activities. Meanwhile, voting at elections ranks not only as a privilege but also as a duty; where social welfare is at stake, one's votes will be cast accordingly. Of greater consequence than the formal vote is perhaps the informal vote which consists in writing or telephoning or telegraphing or visiting one's congressman or senator or legislator in the interests of desired legislation. Such communications may be suppler instruments of democracy than the franchise. The citizen expresses his opinion on the issues as they arise. He need not wait for an election with its delays and complications.

Understanding one's opponents can be not only a matter of religion. It can also contribute to political effectiveness. More influential than any other factor in the enactment of laws is the temper of the public mind. We must reckon with that temper if we would accomplish social betterment. We cannot remove the obstacles from our path until we understand those obstacles. We cannot deal successfully with the opposition until we know what causes the opposition. We must comprehend the fears, the anxieties, the vexations, and the privations that underlie the opposition. We must, for example, anticipate the resistance of the taxpayer to anything which threatens to increase the tax burden.

Perhaps the most virulent issue of the present hour is that of free enterprise versus government ownership and control. Those who favor a maximum of private enterprise argue, with cogency, that people do their best work when they are free. People are happier when they are free, and therefore more efficient. Whether in art, science, literature, religion, commerce, or industry, people achieve most when they are untrammeled. Meanwhile, those who favor action by the government point out how people, when unrestrained, exploit their employees, ruin their competitors and, at frequent intervals, plunge the entire country into a depression. The terrible depression which raged between 1930 and 1940 is cited as an example of what happens when business does as it pleases. Bind someone's hands, and he is powerless to hurt you; but he is also powerless to help you. Untie his hands, and he is able to help; but he is also able to harm.

This indicates a problem inordinately complex. Here, if anywhere, cocksureness is out of place. The optimum of private enterprise or of public enterprise may vary from land to land and from decade to decade. People of some types might thrive best under public enterprise. Others may thrive best under private enterprise. Here, if anywhere, the inflexible mind is a menace and the adaptable mind a need.

All of these intricacies are further complicated by the fact that every doctrine is not only a program but also a symbol. Protective tariff is not merely a question of rates and prices. It is also a token of the group to which one belongs, in behalf of which one's feelings expand, and against whose antagonists one's feelings bristle. Free trade is not merely something fiscal. It is even more an emblem of one's social aversions and preferences. Every doctrine—political, economic, or religious—is not only a map which one consults but also a flag which one waves. If we have human well-being sincerely at heart, we will not ignore these distinctions.

This defines our reaction to social problems, provided we religionize mutualism and not rivalism. If rivalism invests our religion, nothing but fear of unpleasant consequences need check us in our ruthlessness, be it the ruthlessness of a radical or that of a reactionary. If our religion be that of mutualism, our social outlook will be the flowering of our compassion for distressed humanity, and our actions will be governed entirely by that concern.

CHAPTER SEVEN

Jewish-Christian Relations

OUR RELATIONSHIP with people who are other than Jewish constitutes not the least of the problems confronting us of the Jewish group. Anti-Semitism is the most prevalent of Jewish concerns. Few are the Jewish persons of the old type or of the new type who show much solicitude about the Messiah, the Mission of Israel, Revelation, Resurrection, or anything else theological. By contrast, the number of those anxious about anti-Semitism is enormous. If there be one characteristic which is common to all Jews without being, at the same time, common to all non-Jews, the fear of anti-Semitism is that trait.

1. MEASURES AGAINST ANTI-SEMITISM

In the United States, anti-Semitism is being combatted by no fewer than six large national Jewish organizations. The expenditures of these organizations are approximately six million dollars a year. Nearly all American cities with considerable Jewish populations have their committees of Jewish public relations guarding against outbreaks of anti-Semitism in their localities. When advisable, these committees, with or without the aid of the national organizations, take action in cases of discrimination against Jewish persons in employment, in schools and colleges, and in hotels; also in cases of attacks upon Jewish children by non-Jewish children or of hoodlumism against Jewish stores, synagogues, or cemeteries, or of malicious invectives or insinuations against Jews in the press or from the pulpit or on the platform.

Notorious among the anti-Semitic devices of recent years are the so-called "Protocols of the Elders of Zion." This anti-Semitic document purports to be a program of action whereby the Jews were to overthrow all existing governments and to bring the entire world under Jewish domination. Students of the document have repeatedly proved it to be a plagiarism and a forgery. The elder Henry Ford, of automobile fame, was sufficiently ignorant of this to permit the publishing and the crediting of those slanders by his newspaper, the *Dearborn Independent*. Legal action against Mr. Ford was impossible because American law recognized libel only against individuals, not against groups. Mr. Ford was prevailed upon to desist from his anti-Semitism only after suit for personal calumny was brought against him by Aaron Sapiro, the Jewish organizer of cooperatives for agriculture. The suit was dropped when Mr. Ford admitted his blunder about the "Protocols" and consented to make his newspaper cease its anti-Semitic diatribes. Some years later the "Protocols" were the subject of a lawsuit in Switzerland. Their forgery and falsity was overwhelmingly demon-strated in court.

Anti-Semitism has also been combatted by Christians. The Federal Council of Churches (now called the National Council of Churches) has repeatedly deplored outbreaks of violence and scurrilities against the Jews. Other Christian bodies have done likewise. Steps for curbing anti-Semitism include, further, various measures adopted by Jewish groups for the governing of their own conduct. Some Jewish public relations organizations have been sponsoring occupational codes for Jewish business men. Thus, Jewish clothiers would be encouraged to assemble and to formulate, after free and thorough discussion, principles of upright behavior in their calling; similarly Jewish dealers in discarded metals, Jewish realtors, or Jewish lawyers. The following excerpts from a code for retail dealers in furniture and rugs will serve as an illustration:

We agree not to use high-pressure methods in selling.

We agree not to sell above regular retail prices.

It is unethical and poor business to sell inferior merchandise.

We agree not to sell "used" merchandise as new.

Window displays shall not be deceiving as to price and quality.

Adjustments and refunds will be made promptly and pleasantly.

It is unethical to entice to enter a store those people who have only stopped to look at the window displays.

Written guarantees should contain a correct description of the article sold, and a plain and understandable statement of what the guarantee pledges.

A notable instance of intra-Jewish control arose in a certain midwestern city. A moving-picture theatre announced a coming presentation of the film, "The Birth of a Nation." The Negroes of that city protested against the film as a defamation of their group. The Ministerial Association of the city, moved by friendship for the Negroes, appealed to the manager of the theatre and asked that the film be withdrawn. The manager replied that he would gladly do so if he could, in some way, recoup himself for the two hundred dollars which the film had already cost. The Ministerial Association thereupon solicited some friendly individuals and raised the two hundred dollars. The film did not appear.

It happened, however, that the manager of the theater was a Jew. A committee of the Jewish Community Council called upon the manager and readily induced him to forego the compensation. It was near Christmas when this happened. With Christmas greetings, the donations were returned to their respective contributors. That the step redounded to the satisfaction of all concerned hardly needs telling.

Anti-Semitism has also been subjected to scientific inquiry. Notable here are the five volumes, *Studies in Prejudice*, sponsored by the American Jewish Committee, edited by Dr. Max Horkheimer and Dr. Samuel H. Flowerman, and written by outstanding psychologists and sociologists.

More recently, Rabbi Henry E. Kagan experimented with methods of allaying anti-Semitism among certain groups of Christian students. The students belonged to classes which Rabbi Kagan had been invited to teach in some Christian summer schools. The Rabbi found that, as a neutralizer of anti-Semitism, free and frank discussion of the students' personal antipathies to Jews was far more effective than impersonal lectures about Jewish ideals and Jewish contributions to civilization.

2. JEWISH-CHRISTIAN FRIENDSHIP

The standard American practice has long been that of courtesy and amenity between non-Jew and Jew. Exchange of pulpits between Protestant preachers and Jewish preachers is common. Frequently Christian audiences are addressed by Jewish speakers and Jewish audiences by Christian speakers. The Jewish Chautauqua Society supplies Jewish lecturers to hundreds of colleges, while the Institutes on Judaism for Christian clergymen, conducted either by the Union of American Hebrew Congregations or by local congregations, have enabled thousands of Christian ministers to acquire some Jewish learning. The Hebrew Union College has, for years, been holding exchange lectureships with certain Christian seminaries, Jewish scholars sharing their knowledge with Christians and Christian scholars with Jews. Jewish women join with Christian women in their annual Day of Prayer. For many years, the period between the birthday of Lincoln and the birthday of Washington has been known as Brotherhood Week or Good Will Week devoted to gatherings of Jews, Catholics, and Protestants, addressed by friendly speakers representing all three faiths. The promotion of Brotherhood Week is a project of the National Conference of Christians and Jews, an organization started in 1928 for the purpose of fostering kindly relations and removing occasions for friction among the three denominations. A few Rabbis have, of late, been questioning the efficacy of these good will ventures. Some Rabbis contend that the initiative is almost one-sidely Jewish, that the only group which expects to benefit is Jewish, and that the results are superficial.

Protestant congregations often hold services in synagogues and Jewish congregations in churches. This happens, as a rule, when some house of worship has been damaged by storm or fire or when some congregation, having abandoned its old structure, has to await the completion of its new structure. Community Chests, almost everywhere, embrace Jewish, Catholic, and Protestant organizations in one alliance, workers and solicitors of each group putting forth their efforts in behalf of all three. Curiously, such joint financing of benevolences, although of recent American origin, was anticipated in Jewish antiquity. An ancient Rabbinic passage reads:

> If some inhabitants of a city are Jewish and some non-Jewish, Jews and non-Jews shall jointly solicit, Jews and non-Jews shall contribute, and the non-Jewish poor as well as the Jewish poor shall be aided (Palestinian Gittin V, 9).

In numerous American communities, Thanksgiving Day union services take place annually and, in these services, Jews participate together with various liberal Protestants, chiefly Unitarians and Universalists. There are even occasions when, out of regard for the Jewish persons present, Protestant ministers use parts of the Jewish prayer book. During the recent war, the United Service Organizations conducted projects in which Jews, Catholics, and Protestants worked together with remarkable harmony. Now and then a chaplain of one faith would minister, in a religious capacity, to men of the other faith. How Rabbis, priests, and pastors have linked their forces in behalf of social justice, we noted in Chapter Six.

Sometimes friction arises over Christmas celebrations in the public schools. Rabbinic associations frown upon such programs; they invoke the oft-used formula about the separation of church and state. Consistently those same Rabbis also oppose the celebrations of Hannukah which have occurred in public schools located in Jewish neighborhoods and attended predominantly by Jewish pupils. Fortunately, uproar over those Christmas celebrations is not frequent. Most Jewish people, Rabbis included, seem to regard those observances as hardly important enough to justify a quarrel. Meanwhile, Jewish participation in Christmas benevolences for the Christian needy marks a most praiseworthy Jewish trait. A converse gesture is that of the Cuyahoga County Child Welfare Board in Cleveland which, annually since 1932, has mailed gracefully ornamented greetings for Hannukah to the Jewish children under its care when it has sent Christmas greetings to the Christian children under its care.

On April 2, 1947, the widely circulating New York newspaper, PM (now no longer published), carried a double-page advertisement, paid for and signed by fifty Protestant clergymen, calling upon their parishioners at Eastertime to abandon the false and wicked accusation that "the Jews killed Christ." Reciprocal was the graciousness of the National Council of Jewish Women in 1945 when it gave to a Negro organization the Council's neighborhood house in the Bronx. This recreational center stood in a locality from which Jewish families were moving out and where Negro families were moving in. The Council of Jewish Women presented not only the building and the equipment but, over and above all that, a subvention of thirty thousand dollars toward the upkeep.

3. THE NEED OF DIFFERENTIATING

There are certain facts regarding Christianity which we who are Jewish must recognize if we would render a fair judgment. One of these is that Christianity displays variety. We have dwelt upon the diversities exhibited by Judaism. The diversities among the Christians are even more numerous, the Christians themselves being more numerous. As there are modernistic phases and antiquated phases of Judaism, so are there modernistic and antiquated phases of Christianity. Certain types of Christianity, like

Greek Orthodoxy or Roman Catholicism, abound in ritual. Among other types, like that of the Quakers, ritual is all but non-existent. Some Christians, like some Jews, cling tenaciously to the old beliefs; while other Christians, like many among the Jews, have supplanted the old beliefs with viewpoints more modern. Some Christians regard all non-Christians with suspicion; others resist prejudice in all of its turns.

Bigotry ignores distinctions. To those who are unfriendly to the Chinese, all Chinese look alike; similarly with those who are hostile to Negroes or to Armenians. Bigotry judges an entire group by the qualities of its most objectionable members. We Jews, who have suffered so much from this, should—of all people—guard against that failing. We should notice that Christianity has many facets. We may be unenthusiastic about the Christian ritual by which, in winter, people are baptized in icy waters. We need not, on that account, withhold commendation from such a magnificent Christian anthem as "Nearer, my God, to Thee" or such an exquisite hymn as "Abide with Me." We may question the claims of some Christian sects that they can heal illness by means of prayer. We need not, for that reason, have reservations about admiring the architecture of Westminster Abbey or of the cathedral at Rheims. Incidentally, there have been Jewish sects also which have practiced out-door immersion in winter and which have held that prayer will cure illness. The Talmud counsels wisely when it bids: "Judge every one in the light of his merits." This can apply also to groups. We can judge any group, Jewish or Christian, Mohammedan or Buddhist, by such of its qualities as impress us favorably. Why base our appraisal only on those traits that excite our displeasure?

4. DIFFERENCES OF "BELIEF"

Nor should we be misled by the differences between Judaism and Christianity in the matter of beliefs. All varieties of belief and disbelief obtain among Christians as they do among Jews. Jews sometimes disagree with their fellow Jews and agree with various Christians, while Christians sometimes disagree with other Christians but agree with some Jews. Modernistic Jewish scholars, for example, regard the first five books of the Bible as the work not of one writer but of numerous writers and of varied and often conflicting schools of thought. In holding this view, those Jewish scholars are in accord with Christian scholars who have reached the same conclusion. Both sets of scholars encounter the opposition of numerous people, both Jewish and Christian, who contend that the first five books of the Bible were written by one man, Moses. Christians who are persuaded that much reported in the New Testament about Jesus is not history but legend, differ from fellow Christians but concur in the findings of learned investigators in our own group. The Jewish novelist, Sholom Asch, was assailed both by Jews and Christians after he published his story about Jesus and later his story about Paul; while Jews as well as Christians were among his defenders.

One is more than likely to stray from the truth if one asserts that Jews believe such and such or that Christians believe such and such. A great deal that goes by the name of belief is not belief at all. It is what psychologists call "verbalization." Some Jews and many Christians profess belief in Divine inspiration. Does anyone possess any clear idea what "Divine" or what "inspiration" means? We speak about the canals on Mars. We may be correct or we may be incorrect; still, certain definite things are indicated by the word "canals" and by the word "Mars." Is there a similarly clear idea when we say "inspiration" or when we say "Divine"? Jews recite: "God is one." Christians recite: "Father, Son, and Holy Ghost." Does either expression convey, to the average person, any thought, at least any clear thought? Is either formula more than a combination of sounds which arouse certain feelings? If various phrases current in churches and synagogues convey no ideas, obviously there are no ideas to combat. All that we can affirm is: "This set of words gives me feelings that are pleasant. That set of words brings me feelings that are unpleasant." It is a matter of taste; and the proverb may be right which declares that "about tastes there can be no disputing."

Of still greater moment is the consideration that beliefs are not detached happenings. A belief of any kind is a token. Beliefs are tokens of the desires by which the beliefs are prompted. It is these desires—not the resultant beliefs—that play the vital roles. A belief may consist of a thoroughly proved and validated scientific conclusion, such as the belief that vaccination is a preventive of smallpox. Such a belief arises from the desire to conquer smallpox as well as from the desire to follow scientific methods—in brief, the desire to possess facts. But the desire for facts is not the only desire that grips the human soul. One may desire to win an election. How often is political belief an eject of such desire? One may desire the exaltation of one's own group over other groups; the outcome may be the belief that one's group is chosen of God. One may desire the discrediting of some hostile group; the upshot can be the belief that the hated ones are doomed to Divine punishment. The desire to escape death may generate the belief in bodily resurrection. All religious beliefs must be judged in this light. Whether or not a belief is in accord with facts is of consequence in science; the very purpose of science is that of satisfying our desire for facts. But the objectives which most people have religionized comprise interests other than that of grasping facts. We may not believe that the star of Bethlehem ever shone. Yet we can appreciate the love that greets a newborn child and recognize the extent to which the tale of Bethlehem may, in the composing or in the repeating, have been projected by such love. We may discredit the Christian story that Jesus ascended into heaven, just as we discredit a similar Jewish story about Elijah. Yet, with the feeling which inspired that story, the feeling that great souls deserve immortality, we may find ourselves in sympathy. We may reject both the Christian and the Jewish doctrines of vicarious atonement—the doctrine that one person's suffering procures the forgiveness of another person's sins; and yet we subscribe to the sentiment which that doctrine embodies, the sentiment that the human soul is so precious as to warrant utmost sacrifice in its behalf.

Much religious belief is akin to art. Raphael paints a cherub. The product is "a thing of beauty" and "a joy forever." Is the worth of that painting vitiated by the circumstance that such an object as a cherub may never have existed? We must bear in mind that the purpose of the painting was not to inform. Its purpose was to delight and inspire. A diagram must comport with facts. A photograph must comport with facts. A painting renders a service other than that of conveying facts. May not the identical feature attach to the doctrines of religion? As statements of fact, they may be inadequate. As works of art—that is, as devices for inspiration and edification—their value may be extraordinary.

A certain Christian woman had suffered a bitter disappointment. With sobs and painful hesitations, she confided her woe to a Jewish friend. Said the Jewish friend: "Think of your Savior in Gethsemane. How stupendous was His grief! How vast was His sorrow! Through this tribulation which has come upon you, your Savior is calling you to share His burden. Recall that hymn which you have so often sung in your church, the hymn with the lines:

> I'll go with Him through the garden,
> I'll go with Him through the garden,
> I'll go with Him through the garden,
> I'll go with Him, with Him all the way.

Go with Him in the garden. Your Savior will sustain you. Your Savior will transform you."

The Christian woman ceased her weeping. Into her face came a look of hope and courage. "Yes," she replied, "Now I see the meaning of it all. I *will* go with Him in the garden. I will live anew in His love." Word soon reached the Jewish friend that the Christian woman had flung off her dejection and had returned to her work with renewed zeal, courage, and success.

Did the Jewish person believe the story which tells how Jesus prayed in the garden of Gethsemane on the night before the crucifixion? Of course not. Did the Jewish person regard Jesus as supernatural, whatever "supernatural" may mean? To be sure, not. Yet how trivial are these points of doctrine by comparison with the need of an anguish-riven heart for sympathy and comfort! The story of Gethsemane may, in its very origin, have been generated by the need for sympathy and comfort. Throughout the ages, that story may have functioned as a token of sympathy and as a device for comfort. All religious doctrines must be approached from that standpoint. We must judge them not by what they communicate but by what they manifest, not by what they allege but by the needs which they fulfill.

5. PROSELYTISM

Christianity has been a missionaristic religion from its inception. The New Testament commands: "Go ye into all the world, and preach the gospel to every creature." Judaism, though a missionaristic religion at certain periods of its history, long ago forsook that tendency. The Orthodox Jewish code strongly discountenances attempts to win converts to Judaism. It enjoins the placing of every obstacle in the way of any non-Jewish person contemplating such a step. The Jewish objection to proselytism is said to have originated in the first century of the Christian era, when converts to Judaism often proved to be spies and saboteurs in the service of the Roman foe. It is otherwise today. Today there are leaders of Judaism who hold that, where Jewish ways of thinking and observing would confer, on an individual, satisfactions not otherwise obtainable, that individual should be welcomed into a Jewish mode of life. These leaders do not actively proselytize but, given certain circumstances, they encourage the adoption of Judaism, in one form or another, by persons who are other than Jewish by birth. A dissenting view contends that the value of such conversions is questionable. Conversion commonly means the exchange of one set of theological beliefs for another. This throws the emphasis upon belief; and some of us feel that this is precisely where the emphasis does not belong. The stressing of belief has not only plunged religion and science into conflict and has not only impeded human progress by fettering human thought; what is more, it has deflected attention from that nobility of conduct and that appreciation of loveliness in which many of us find religion at its best.

Converts to Judaism have been obligated, even by Jewish liberals, not only to "believe" certain things but also to "study" certain things. The convert is expected to acquire certain Jewish learning. How strange to demand of a convert what we do not demand of people who are Jewish by birth! It may be desirable or admirable for a Jewish person to study Jewish history, literature, ideas, rituals, and practices. But compulsion to pursue such studies lies entirely outside of our usage. Excepting professors in Jewish colleges and Rabbis, few Jewish people of American nativity possess Jewish knowledge. How inappropriate to require of a convert what we do not require of ourselves!

It is nearly always for the purpose of marriage to Jewish persons that non-Jewish persons become "converted." If, owing to pressure from the older generation, such "conversion" proves inescapable, why should it not suffice merely to have the non-Jewish person make some formal declaration of willingness to be called a Jew or a Jewess and to accept all the consequences of being thus called? The chief consequences would be solicitation for Jewish benevolences and for membership in Jewish organizations, plus perhaps some exposure to discrimination and persecution at certain times and places. No convert should be constrained to believe, to practice, or to study along lines unusual in the Jewish milieu itself.

Conversions of Jewish people to Christianity are rare, at least in the United States. When such conversions occur, the Jewish reaction is sometimes one of regret or even of hostility. Jews who make the transition are, in Jewish circles, commonly accused of mercenary motives. There may be cases in which that imputation is warranted. But how do we know? Were it not better to heed the Talmudic adage about forbearing to pass judgment on people until we understand their circumstances?

To sum up: If we would cope with prejudice, our first step must be that of forswearing prejudice in our own attitudes. We must ourselves remain clean of prejudice, be it prejudice against Orthodox Jews or against Catholics or against any group whatsoever. Prejudice is rivalism. Prejudice is vindictiveness. Certain beliefs or practices, which differ from our own, affront our Ego (see page 78); and prejudice amounts to a form of revenge. By means of prejudice, we retaliate for what our Ego suffers. Prejudice and mutualism stand at opposite poles. If mutualism be our ideal, prejudice will be our abhorrence.

CHAPTER EIGHT

War and Peace

CONSPICUOUS AMONG the life problems which all of us have to confront is the problem of war and peace. There is not one of us whose future is unaffected by our country's decisions in that regard. For those of us who are liable to military service, war is literally a matter of life and death. For all of us, it is a question of poverty or plenty. No matter what our plans, they are at the mercy of war and of war preparations.

Opinions on this subject, though many and varied, admit of two broad classifications. A person is either a pacifist or a non-pacifist. Pacifists hold that war is never justifiable. Non-pacifists maintain that war is sometimes justifiable and necessary. Everywhere pacifists form a scant minority. America is distinctly a non-pacifistic nation. When tempers flare, non-pacifists brand pacifists as traitors, while pacifists retort: "War-mongers!" Both appellatives are unfair. Pacifists are not traitors and non-pacifists are not war-mongers. Pacifists can be patriotic, and non-pacifists can be sincerely desirous of peace. Though their methods may at points diverge, the two groups need differ not at all in their dedication to the cause of peace. To both groups belong people of intelligence, honor, and good will. Occasionally pacifists and non-pacifists join forces. Pacifists cooperate with non-pacifists in the undertaking of war time succor and relief—such as the work of the Red Cross. Non-pacifists have allied themselves with pacifists in disapproval of peace time conscription, in opposition to military training in colleges, and in support of the law which, in the days of our neutrality, forbade our selling of arms to belligerents.

Pacifists and non-pacifists agree that war is the extreme of cruelty. Everyone concedes that war and mutualism are utterly incompatible. The Central Conference of American Rabbis once declared that "war is a denial of all for which religion stands." The Rabbis meant, of course, religion of the mutualistic kind (see pages 33, 34). Christians pronounce war the antithesis of Christianity—of Christianity, needless to say, in its altruistic sense. For all that, people have contrived to reconcile religion and war. They explain that, when a foe threatens, a situation exists in which religion becomes inapplicable. One's first duty is that of defending one's country. Only after the foe has been vanquished, will religion again have pertinence, according to this view. Otherwise the relation between war and religion poses no problem; for religion can embody rivalism as well as mutualism (page 35). Where war itself has been religionized, the national defense associated with war has, in all ages and climes, acquired religious sanction.

1. PACIFISM

The pacifist maintains that war does not defend. Says the pacifist: "Those who speak of war as national defense do so on the assumption that their side is going to win. But what assurance have we that our side is going to win? Every war is a gamble. Every belligerent enters the war expecting victory. One side will lose. The losing side may be ours. Then," asks the pacifist, "what becomes of our national defense? The defeated side has to bear not only the losses and the privations of the war itself but has, in addition, to endure the reparations and the retributions imposed by the conqueror."

Even the victor, according to the pacifist, is not defended. Persons informed about atomic energy warn us that, from an atomic war, no victor will emerge. From an atomic war, nothing can ensue but widespread death and devastation. Our civilian defense program virtually anticipates such devastation. Albert

Einstein, one of the discoverers of atomic energy, has predicted that, if World War III is fought with atomic bombs, World War IV will be fought with clubs. That is to say, men will be back at savagery, back in the jungle, back to where man was before civilization began. "Would that be national defense?" asks the pacifist.

Granting, nonetheless, that we survive and that we win, have we, even then, been defended? The pacifist answers: "The slain and the maimed have surely not been defended, even among the victors. The wives robbed of their husbands, the children deprived of their fathers, the parents bereaved of their sons have hardly been defended. The victims of crushing taxes and of gigantic inflation, of harrowing scarcities and of merciless crowding, of interrupted careers and of disorganized homes have assuredly not been defended. Those who suffer from the infringements upon civil liberties which follow in the wake of war and of war preparations have also not been defended"—argues the pacifist.

The pacifist reminds us that, in the second world war, one of the victors was Great Britain. But the war-wrought sufferings of Britain have been such that Britons have questioned whether their country's plight could have been worse had Britain been not a victor but a loser. Most of us Jews, during World War II, were citizens of the victorious countries and supporters of the victorious belligerents. Yet six million Jews were slain and a million and a half made homeless. From the fighting front in Italy, an American war correspondent cabled to his newspaper in the United States: "Wars are won by those who do not wage them, and that nation prospers which keeps its youth alive." How the pacifist applauds those words!

At the time of the first world war, we were told that our victory would make the world safe for democracy. We won. Did the world become safe for democracy? Democracy suffered a setback from which it has not yet begun to recover. We were told, at the time of the second world war, that once we had vanquished our foe, all would be well. Then, at the very pinnacle of our triumph, the very persons who had promised us security warned us that now our peril was greater than it had ever been before.

That is what the pacifist means when he says that wars do not defend. The pacifist also pleads that preparedness does not defend. We often hear it asserted that, if we are sufficiently armed, war will be prevented. No nation will dare molest us. We shall be in a position to maintain the peace of the world. The pacifist would reply to this: "Why not use some imagination? When another nation arms, does it make us less inclined to fight that nation or more inclined? Does not that other nation's armament goad us to 'get at' that nation in order to remove the menace?" The pacifist asks: "Why should it be otherwise if the arming is done by us? Our armament produces not concessiveness in other nations; it produces counter-armament. Our armament makes other nations not eager to spare us but eager to annihilate us."

Pacifists further point out that armament is colossally expensive. Its costs soar into billions. And armament becomes rapidly outdated. New inventions are constantly arising which put existing armament behind the times. Tremendous is the temptation to use this expensive panoply before it grows obsolete. The result is that war is not prevented; war is precipitated.

2. THE PACIFIST'S NATIONAL DEFENSE

Meanwhile the pacifist proposes what he regards as a genuine national defense. The pacifist likens a nation to an individual. The individual is safe when among his friends. Among his foes, an individual is imperiled no matter how many his weapons. The way to defend America is to render America so beloved by all nations that all will wish to bless her and none to do her harm. If America would so deport herself toward other nations that none can hurt America without hurting its best of friends, that none can injure America without *ipso facto* injuring itself, then, according to the pacifist, would America be safe. According to the pacifist, there is no national defense except international amity. If the billions we spend on war were devoted to feed the starving, to clothe the tattered, to shelter the homeless, to employ the jobless, to heal the sick, to train the unskilled, wherever they might be in the world, then would America be safe. If the genius of a Roosevelt or a Hopkins, an Eisenhower or a MacArthur were employed not to destroy human life but to enhance human life, then would America be well defended. Such is the pacifistic doctrine.

Eighteen hundred years ago, a Jewish sage raised the question: "Who is a hero?" His answer was: "A hero is he who subjugates his own inclinations." In a later generation, another Jewish teacher, discussing that definition of a hero, asked another question. That later sage queried: "Who is the hero of heroes?" Who is the supreme hero? Who is the consummate hero? His answer was: "The hero of heroes is he who changeth a foe into a friend" (Abot de Rabbi Nathan 23). The well protected nation, according to the pacifist, would, in like vein, be the nation which changes its foe into a friend.

How can we change a foe into a friend? A well known book carries the title, *How to Make Friends and Influence People*. There are several books on that theme. All of them agree that, to win a friend, we must avoid threatening and avoid menacing. We must forego upbraiding, scolding, and fault-finding. We must be tactful. We must omit mentioning that person's flaws. We must dwell upon that person's excellences. All of which is the very opposite of what prevails when friction arises between nations. Everything favorable in each nation is then ignored by the other. Everything unfavorable is then stressed by the other. That is not the way in which to change a foe into a friend. We should seek out such qualities in our foe as can evoke our approval. These we must emphasize and not that which is derogatory—says the pacifist—if we would change our foe into a friend.

International trade also helps change a foe into a friend. Some-one has observed that, if goods do not cross boundary lines, soldiers will. If a nation can procure by purchase that which it needs, there remains scant inducement to incur the frightful expense of war in order to obtain what it needs. The levelling of immigration barriers would also help change a foe into a friend. Relieving a country of its excess population can constitute assistance of a substantial kind. Another device for changing a foe into a friend would be President Truman's Point Four, that is, monetary and technical aid to underprivileged nations enabling them to develop their resources. Such are the expedients for national defense which appeal to the pacifist.

3. THE PSYCHOLOGY OF WAR

The pacifist reminds us that, during any war and for a time preceding a war, all information regarding the foe comes to us distorted. Our channels of publicity permit us to hear only that which will, by enraging us, quicken our will to fight. Once the war is over, it gradually comes to light that many deprecatory things which we said about the foe, like many of the deprecatory things which the foe said about us, were untrue. In every war, according to a certain British statesman, "truth is the first casualty." The suppositions on which people have gone to war have, again and again in human history, turned out to be erroneous.

To convey an untruth, it is not even necessary to devise a false statement. Our biggest lies can consist not in what we say but in what we omit. We can dilate on the atrocities of the enemy and conceal the fact that our own side could not keep clean of atrocities in like situations. We can leave out of account every extenuating or even explanatory circumstance connected with the enemy's doings.

The pacifist believes that we could have achieved our independence from Great Britain without any war. Our difficulties with Mexico and, fifty years later, with Spain could, even according to *non*-pacifist historians, have been abated without war. Students of the Southern secession apprise us that slavery could have been abolished and the Union preserved without war. Little doubt exists today that methods other than war could have relieved the strains which, from 1914 to 1918, cost such prodigious loss of life, treasure, and freedom. While we are still too close to the second world war to grasp its implications, it is highly significant that our foes of a few years ago have already become our friends and that some friends of a few years ago are today our foes.

Not the least of the factors which move the pacifist to deny the necessity for war is the circumstance that, in all wars of our time, both sides employ the same slogans. Both sides claim to be fighting for national defense. Each side insists that its very survival is at stake. Both sides step forth as champions of democracy. Each side execrates the other as the aggressor. What President Wilson observed about the first world war might apply to any war. Said President Wilson: "The objects, which the statesmen of the belligerents on both sides have in mind in this war, are virtually the same." Why should either side go to war if its objects, or at least its ideals, are so fully compatible with those of its opponents? To be sure, each side accuses the other of insincerity. But if that charge is valid for one, why may it not prove equally valid for the other? And what remains of a nation's justification for war if the reasons it advances are insincere and not genuine? For the pacifist, these become vital considerations.

Those who are at all familiar with modern psychology may question whether, in case of war, national defense is, at all, the motive. National defense can be not a reason but a rationalization (page 54). The real reason for war may be, like much else in human affairs, something unexpressed or unconscious. One noted psychologist traces the war urge to the infantilisms which linger in our psyche long after we have become adult. This psychologist writes:

To understand human nature, we must realize that human beings usually function on two levels: one mature and rational, the other infantile and egocentric. It's the basically childish attitude of seeing other people as potential rivals and sources of danger that arouses the hostility which leads to wars, and if we could educate the mass of mankind to see one another from a mature standpoint—that is, as having essential interests in common—we could have peace (Dr. Leon J. Saul in *The Psychoanalytic Quarterly,* quoted by Lawrence Gould in "Mirror of Your Mind," January 31, 1950).

In 1939, the Yale Institute of Human Relations published a book entitled *Frustration and Aggression* by John Dollard and others, which adduces clinching evidence that, every time a person is thwarted, that person craves revenge. If, as often happens, the thwarted person can not inflict his revenge on the real cause of his grievance, he contents himself with a scapegoat. He chooses a substitute. He directs his anger against someone who has nothing to do with his annoyance—like the man who, reprimanded by his employer yet not daring to talk back to his employer, comes home and vents his exasperation on his wife and children. For substitutions of this kind, the technical word is "displacement." People, displacing their many chagrins, sometimes assail various groups such as Negroes, Catholics, Jews, immigrants, capitalists, "Wall Street," Communists, and the like. When the proper hour strikes, they displace their woes upon the Kaiser or Hitler or Stalin. Such, rather than national defense, would, as the pacifist sees it, generate the real impulsion to war.

Then there are the encomiums bestowed on the men in the armed services, especially on those who lose their lives. The eulogies lavished on the heroes who died or who dared for their country obscure an all-important fact—namely, that in the disablement or the death of a hero, the country loses; it does not gain. A healthy, capable, and upright man serves his country not by perishing but by living. A man's country is benefited when his powers are put to work, not when they are impaired or destroyed. If, as the pacifist contends, the fighting does not protect the country but imperils the country, those reflections become overwhelmingly pertinent.

4. THE VIEWS OF THE NON-PACIFISTS

Those were the ponderings of the pacifists. Little need exists for setting forth the other view. Every newspaper in the land and every broadcast dealing with international affairs propounds the non-pacifistic approach. Every school in the land, every synagogue in the land and, with meager exceptions, every church in the land articulates non-pacifistic convictions. All teach that war is needed for national defense and that armament is indispensable if we would deter other nations from aggressing.

5. THE JEWISH ANGLE

Within the framework which we have sketched, we now consider our subject from the standpoint of Judaism. On the theme of world peace, the ancient Jewish writings contain some famous utterances, some of which we have already noted (page 39):

He shall judge between the nations,
And shall decide from many peoples;
And they shall beat their swords into ploughshares
And their spears into pruning-hooks;
Nation shall not lift up sword against nation,
Neither shall they learn war any more
(Isaiah 2.4; Micah 4.3).

I will break the bow and the sword and the
battle out of the land (Hosea 2.20).

He maketh wars to cease unto the ends of the earth;
He breaketh the bow and cutteth the spear in sunder;
He burneth the chariots in fire (Psalm 46.10).

The word of the Lord came unto me (David) saying: Thou
hast shed blood abundantly, and hast made great wars; thou
shalt not build a house unto My name, because thou hast
shed much blood upon the earth in my sight
(I Chronicles 22.8).

From the post-biblical writings, the writings of the Rabbis, we glean sentiments such as these:

> One man was created the common ancestor of all so that the various families of men should not contend with one another (Sanhedrin 38A).

> God found for Israel no surer vehicle of blessing than peace (Ukzin III, 12).

> Great is peace; for all blessings are contained therein.
> Great is peace; for all Divine commands are connected therewith.
> Great is peace; for, when King Messiah cometh, his beginning will be peace (Numbers Rabbah XI. 16).

The passage in Exodus 20.22 which forbids the use of iron in the construction of the altar is rabbinically interpreted to signify that iron is out of place at the altar, because iron is the metal of strife, while the altar stands for peace between "man and man, family and family, nation and nation" (Mekilta Jethro 25. Sifra Kedoshim XI.8).

There can be no disputing that these expressions manifest mutualism. They bespeak the mutualistic trends which Judaism religionized ages ago (see page 36). For all that, we can not class these sayings as pacifistic. To that which they assert, pacifists and non-pacifists can equally subscribe. Those passages, though envisaging peace as an ideal, neither affirm nor deny the non-pacifistic contention that war is indispensable for national defense.

In the book of Jeremiah, by contrast, there are passages which, referring to the Babylonians besieging Jerusalem, read like counsels of non-resistance:

> And it shall come to pass, that the nation and the kingdom which will not serve the same Nebuchadnezzar king of Babylon, and that will not put their neck under the yoke of the King of Babylon, that nation will I visit, saith the Lord, with the sword, and with famine, and with pestilence, until I have consumed them by his hand . . . But the nation that shall bring their neck under the yoke of the king of Babylon, and serve him, that nation will I let

remain in their own land, saith the Lord; and they shall till it, and dwell therein (Jeremiah 27.8, 11).

There are similar thoughts in Jeremiah 38.14-27. It has been surmised that these pacifistic strands in Jeremiah are not the words of Jeremiah but the words of an interpolator who misunderstood Jeremiah. Be that as it may, an Old Testament writer—if not Jeremiah, then an interpolator of Jeremiah—did have ideas akin to those of modern pacifists.

Also of pacifistic tenor is the response of Isaac when the Philistines rob him of his laboriously dug wells. Every time the Philistines drive Isaac's herdsmen away from one of Isaac's wells, Isaac patiently digs another well. Eventually the Philistines desist from their seizures. The King of the Philistines himself honors Isaac with a visit of apology and peace. Then God appears unto Isaac. "Fear not, I am with thee, and will bless thee" are the divine words to the forbearing, non-resistant man (Genesis 26.24).

A verse much loved by pacifists is that in Zechariah 4.6: "Not by might nor by power, but by My spirit, saith the Lord of hosts." In its context, however, the verse refers not to any external military action but to political assaults upon a certain Jewish leader, Zerubbabel, by his own compatriots.

Cognate to these are the expressions of international good will which were quoted in a previous chapter (page 39). We might amplify these with that passage from Amos, the first of the literary prophets:

Are ye not as the children of the Ethiopians unto Me,
O children of Israel? Saith the Lord.
Have not I brought up Israel out of the land of Egypt,
And the Philistines from Caphtor,
And Aram from Kir? (Amos 9.7).

The Ethiopians were Negroes. In the days of Amos, as today, there were those who looked down upon Negroes as inferiors. Amos makes short shrift of that notion. In the sight of God, according to Amos, Hebrew and Ethiopian, white and black, are alike. The

Philistines whom Amos mentions were Israel's ancient foes. The wars between the Hebrews and the Philistines were numerous and bloody. The Arameans were likewise Israel's ancient foes. Between the Hebrews and the Arameans, the wars were frequent and gory. But the prophet, mentioning precisely those fierce adversaries of the Hebrews, proclaims that, before God, all nations are alike. According to the prophet, God does not take sides. God stands above the strife.

This does not deny that numerous passages in the Bible contemplate war with approval. Consider, for instance, these words from the eighteenth Psalm (verses 39-43):

> I have smitten them through, so that
>   they are not able to rise;
> They are fallen under my feet.
> For Thou hast girded me with strength unto the battle;
> Thou hast subdued under me those that rose up against me.
> Thou hast also made mine enemies turn their backs unto me,
> And I did cut off them that hate me.
> They cried, but there was none to save;
> Even unto the Lord, but He answered them not.
> Then did I beat them small as the dust before the wind;
> I did cast them out as the mire of the streets.

The Bible abounds in such enthusiastic accounts of battles. Despite its great outpourings on the subject of peace, one can hardly maintain that the Bible is a pacifistic literature.

Unique in the Old Testament is a position which might be described as one midway between the two views. We refer to the thought that, while war may be advantageous, it is not man but God that does the fighting. Thus the account in Exodus 14.14 represents Moses as announcing: "The Lord will fight for you; and ye shall hold your peace." The Psalmist avers:

> Some trust in chariots, and some in horses;
> But we will make mention of the name of the
>   Lord our God (Psalm 20, 8).

Isaiah rebukes King Ahaz for taking military steps against the invading foes (Isaiah 7). The prophet declares that the defense of the country should be left to God, not to the contrivances of human beings. That thought occurs in the Old Testament repeatedly. The doctrine favors destructive treatment of the enemy; at the same time, in the manner of pacifism, it would deter people from war.

Closer than the Bible to the pacifistic persuasion are the writings of the Rabbis who lived long after the Bible was completed. It is curious, indeed amusing, how the Jewish teachers of that later day speak about the Bible's military heroes as if they were not heroes of the battlefield but heroes of the schoolroom. Joshua, Caleb, David, Benaiah, and other biblical warriors are represented by the Rabbis as being not military men but students, scholars, and bookmen like the Rabbis themselves.

The Rabbis labor also to transmute the military tone of the Bible into the opposite sentiment. We have already noticed (page 40) how that bellicose fifth chapter of the Book of Judges is made the occasion of furthering kindness, gentleness, and forbearance:

> They who are reviled but revile not others, they who hear themselves reproached but make no reply, they whose every act is one of love and who cheerfully bear their afflictions—these are the ones of whom Scripture saith: 'They that love Him be as the sun when he goeth forth in his might.'

The terminal sentence of that saintly utterance is quoted from that raving biblical war song.

Similar is a homily based on the Song of the Red Sea (Exodus 15). In this song, Israel exults at the drowning of its Egyptian pursuers. A Rabbi Jonathan, who lived in the third century of the Christian era, narrates that when, seeing the Egyptian foe drown, Israel burst forth into paeans of triumph, the angels up in heaven began to join Israel in its jubilation. But this provoked a Divine rebuke (Megillah 10B). Said God: "The work of my hands are drowning, and ye would sing a song?" Is not such a fancy nearer to pacifism than to non-pacifism?

The Jewish historian Josephus tells of a renowned saint by the name of Onias who, in the course of a civil war, was seized by an army which was attacking Jerusalem. The captors of Onias commanded him to pray that they might be divinely favored with victory. It cost Onias his life when he supplicated:

O God, king of the whole world, since those that stand now with me are Thy people, and those that are besieged are also Thine, I beseech Thee that Thou wilt neither hearken to the prayers of those against these, nor bring to effect what these pray against those (Antiquities, XIV-2-1).

It is also recorded that, just prior to the downfall of Judea in the year 70 of the Christian era, a Jewish statesman and a noted Rabbi pleaded for non-resistance to the Romans. The statesman was King Agrippa. Josephus ascribes to Agrippa a speech of amazing eloquence. One of the sentences in that speech reads:

Nothing so much damps the force of strokes as bearing them with patience; and the quietness of those who are injured diverts the injurious persons from afflicting (Jewish War, II-16-351).

The famed teacher who implored the people to refrain from war was Johanan ben Zakkai. "How long will you do this, slaying the world with famine?" asks Rabbi Johanan ben Zakkai as he reproves the leader of those who were agitating for war (Gittin 56A). Nor did Johanan lack the support of his Rabbinic colleagues. An entire group of Rabbis urged: "Let us make peace with them" (*Ibid.*). It was Johanan ben Zakkai who, utilizing the high regard in which he was held by the Romans, established the school through which Judaism, all but annihilated by war, was preserved and perpetuated by the processes of peace.

As we have already stated, our opinions can not be a repetition of opinions expressed long ago and far away. The ancient Jewish writings embody opposing points of view. Even if they did not, even if the Jewish writings were uniformly pacifistic or uniformly non-pacifistic, even then, their conclusions can not dictate our conclusions. Each one of us, in accordance with his or her temperament, experiences, and education, must arrive at the convictions which he or she will cherish.

There exists at present a tiny organization of Jewish pacifists. It is called the Jewish Peace Fellowship. This society seeks, by means of pacifism, to emphasize the mutualistic strains in Jewish teaching. Yet, by and large, the Jewish outlook, like the Christian outlook, is non-pacifistic. The majority of Jews, like the majority of Christians, are non-pacifistic. Jews deem it to their credit and to their advantage that they can point to the extensiveness of Jewish participation in the wars of our country. Some Jews propound the argument that Jewish pacifism might furnish grist for anti-Semitism. And this non-pacificism has been strengthened by two recent occurrences. One was the struggle against Hitler; the other was the strife between the Zionists and the Arabs at the founding of the State of Israel. Because of Hitler or because of the Israel-Arab conflict or because of both, Jewish attitudes at the present hour tend, as never before, to reject pacifism.

6. OUR OWN PART

Faced by these bewilderments, what should be our own line of action? One rule should be: Obey the law. Whether we are pacifists or non-pacifists, we should respect the law. Pacifists sometimes fail to register for the armed services or to arrive at assigned camps or to carry out orders issued at camp, despite the latitude granted to conscientious objectors by the laws of America. Some pacifists refuse to pay their taxes, or at least that percentage of their taxes which corresponds to the percentage of its budget that the government expends for war. Non-pacifists have flouted the law by assaulting conscientious objectors or by disturbing pacifist assemblies. Sometimes defiance of the law is applauded by reputable and respected members of the community. With what admiration people speak of the Boston Tea Party or of the Storming of the Bastille or of the Underground Railroad, that organized arrangement for assisting slaves to escape from their Southern masters! All of these involved the breaking of the law. Every religion acclaims its martyrs; and martyrs are ever so often defiers of the law. To invoke the "law of God," some kind of "higher" law superseding the law of the state, is but a pious way of claiming immunity to laws which one happens to oppose.

We should not violate or encourage others to violate the law. Laws should be obeyed even if they are objectionable. If it is right to violate a law because one is opposed to that law, then it would be right for the bootlegger or the rent-gouger or the black-marketeer to violate the law. The way in which to cope with an offensive law is not to violate it but to avert it or repeal it by orderly democratic processes. A president of the United States once said: "To get rid of a bad law, enforce it." We might add: "To get rid of a bad law, obey it." Not those who break the laws but those who heed the laws are likely to wield influence when bad laws are to be prevented or removed.

Another requisite would be compunction about our state of mind. The controversies between pacifists and non-pacifists can generate much odium. Each side comes to hold the other in contempt. Here, as elsewhere, the Ego bound up with one's opinion becomes painfully lacerated when that opinion is assailed (page 78). Such hateful reactions are the antithesis of mutualism. If mutualism be our ideal, our spells of detestation collide with our ideal. Scornful feelings engendered by the conflict between pacifism and non-pacifism are no better than scornful feelings due to any other causes. If we favor mutualism, those feelings can not be condoned.

Elections, as they occur at present, offer little opportunity to vote for or against war. The major parties are unreservedly non-pacifistic. In most states, no matter how one votes, one votes for candidates and platforms that deem war, at times, unavoidable. The ordinary citizen's main channel of political expression consists in petitioning one's congressman or one's senators. The letter or the telegram to one's representatives at Washington is a far more pliable instrument of democracy than the ballot. This, it is believed, was the device which recently defeated Universal Military Training. We must not, of course, overestimate the significance of this defeat from the standpoint of pacifism. Opposition to Universal Military Training is not opposition to war. Universal Military Training was rejected on the ground of its expense and its inconvenience; the training was not regarded as a menace to the nation's security. While a communication to our representatives in Congress is our best and, for most of us, our only way of influencing public affairs, pacifists must remember that the vast majority of communications reaching Congress will not be of a pacifistic tenor. Most of the people who write to Congress are not pacifists. Congress is most likely to hear from those who believe that, at times, war is imperative.

Our soundest recourse is hope, that hope which has become religionized. Not only evil but also good has its place in the universe. What our sacred literature calls trusting in the Lord has never proved futile. Many a problem attains solution in ways unsurmised and unanticipated. Such an unsurmised and unanticipated solution may yet put an end to the problem of war. Here again there may await us that deliverance which is for us the meaning of God our Redeemer.

CHAPTER NINE

Life Everlasting

DIFFERING FROM various Christian circles which accord great prominence to the belief in a hereafter, Jewish sentiment tends to assign that doctrine a subordinate place. The reasons for this difference may be varied. So far as we ourselves are concerned, a possible factor may be the anti-scientific spirit in which the subject is commonly handled. In discussions of a hereafter, occultism, obscurantism, and wishful thinking often play an inordinate role.

Yet an honest and responsible approach to the question of a hereafter may prove welcome. The fear of death is, like eating and breathing, one of our biological functions. An organism must stave off death if it is to exist at all. To persevere in warding off death, the organism must abhor death. That is why the abhorrence of death had to become fixed in the organism by natural selection.

This does not gainsay that there may also lodge, in the organism, trends to the contrary. Psychoanalysis speaks of a "death wish." Suicide is probably, in some sense, a fulfilment of the death wish. Death is often craved by people when suffering intense pain; the modern Euthanasia movement recognizes that fact. "Euthanasia" means "mercy-killing" medically performed under legal safeguards. If Euthanasia were lawful, the physician, when duly authorized by a court, would be permitted to induce an easy death for a patient who, because of intense and unrelievable suffering, asks that impending dissolution be hastened. The philosopher Nietzsche aptly wrote: "Pain saith 'perish!'" This may also account for what clergymen report when they tell of dying people who anticipate death with serenity. Clergymen impute that serenity to a belief in a hereafter. That explanation is, of course, impaired by the consideration that myriads of people, though they believe in a hereafter, stand nonetheless in nameless terror of death.

Medical history knows of a Filipino leader, José Rizal (1861-1896) who was put to death by the Spaniards. A physician who took the condemned man's pulse just before the execution reported the pulse to have been that of a person utterly calm and unperturbed. There may be situations in which any of us would lose the fear of death; for example if, by sacrificing our life, we could save the life of a child.

A noted psychologist, who was himself averse to a belief in a hereafter, once wrote that this belief appeals especially to youth. He regarded the belief as a sublimation of the youthful urge to perpetuate the race. This psychologist could have added that the fear of death possesses for youth a virulence which it loses in later years. While the fear of death may or may not yield to a belief in a hereafter, that fear can readily make the question of a hereafter one of profound concern.

1. THE ATTITUDE OF THE JEWISH PAST

The Old Testament has little to say about a life beyond the grave. The Old Testament is occupied all but exclusively with the world of our present existence. In an old Jewish hymnal, a hymn for the Feast of Weeks contains the stanza:

> Thy word explains the joys and pains
> The soul on earth that trieth.
> It calls this life a scene of strife
> To gain what never dieth.

The Bible does indeed concern itself with this earth and does indeed depict it as a scene of strife. Also included in the Bible are deep spiritual insights for which "what never dieth" may be an appropriate phrase. What we may question is whether, in the Bible, life's pains and joys are explained. In the Bible, life's pains and joys

115

are recognized. Explaining is a function of science; and for science the world had to wait until modern times.

There are passages in the Bible which specifically deny personal immortality:

If a man die, shall he live again? (Job 14.14).

The dead shall not praise the Lord (Psalm 115.17).

The dead live not, the shades rise not (Isaiah 26.14).

> As the cloud is consumed and vanisheth away,
> So he that goeth down to the grave
> Shall come up no more (Psalm 88.5).

In death there is no remembrance of Thee (Psalm 6.5).

Before I go hence, and be no more (Psalm 39.14).

The only immortality envisaged by the Bible as a whole is the immortality of the people Israel. Even this immortality meets with denial in the utterances of Amos, Isaiah, and perhaps others of the prophets. The Bible is a living demonstration that the belief in a hereafter is not essential to religion.

The Bible does, at one place, speak about the ghost of the deceased prophet, Samuel (I Samuel 28). The witch of En-dor announces to King Saul that she sees the ghost. King Saul, who has consulted the witch, does not see the ghost; he merely hears it speak. Necromancy is mentioned in the Bible at various places, usually as something outlawed (Leviticus 19.31; 20.27; I Samuel 28.9; Isaiah 8.19; 29.4). The story of Elijah in the Bible alleges that Elijah's life on earth terminated with his flying to heaven in a celestial chariot and that Elisha, his chief disciple, beheld the ascension (II Kings, 2). Significantly, the other disciples do not credit Elisha's account. For three days, a searching party scours the hills. The text does not state whether their failure to find Elijah convinced them that an ascension had really occurred. In later literature, a similar ascension was imputed to Enoch, mentioned in Genesis 4.24. The early Christians adopted this pattern in their story of Jesus. Such also is perhaps the sense of verse twenty-four in that spiritually exalted seventy-third Psalm:

> Thou wilt guide me with Thy counsel,
> And afterward receive me to glory.

The expression in Ecclesiastes 12.7,

> And the dust returneth to the earth as it was,
> And the spirit returneth unto God who gave it,

though used in modern rituals as if it affirmed the immortality of the soul, is not thus understood by modern commentators. "Spirit" here is said to mean merely the breath. The thought is that, while the dust goes down to the earth, the departing breath proceeds in the opposite direction.

Twice does the Bible, in very late passages, affirm the resurrection of the body. One of these passages is Daniel 12.2:

> And many of them that sleep in the dust shall awake.

The other passage is Isaiah 26.19:

> Thy dead shall live, my dead bodies shall arise . . .
> And the earth shall bring to life the shades.

However, this latter passage may be intended merely as a metaphor for the revival of the dormant nation, like the dry bones which come together and form living bodies in Ezekiel, chapter thirty-seven.

In the Talmud and other post-Biblical writings, the doctrine of bodily resurrection is asserted repeatedly. The doctrine has found its way into the Orthodox Jewish prayer book:

> In the abundance of His kindness God will revive the dead.

> Thou art mighty forever, O Lord, Thou quickenest the dead . . . Yea, faithful art Thou to quicken the dead. Blessed art Thou, O Lord, who quickenest the dead.

> My God, the soul which Thou hast given me is pure . . . Thou wilt take it from me, but wilt restore it unto me hereafter . . .
> Blessed art Thou, O Lord, who restorest souls unto dead bodies.

The resurrection of dead bodies was expected to occur in a coming millenium or golden age of the Messiah. Wicked people, such as usurers for instance, were to be debarred from the resurrection; but, in the resurrection, all of the righteous, whether Jewish or non-Jewish, were to have a share.

In some isolated localities, there are people—Jewish as well as Catholic and Protestant—who still believe in bodily resurrection. Otherwise the doctrine has been abandoned. It has been discarded even by those who, with or without understanding the Hebrew, recite the prayers in which that belief is professed. Nowadays people who accept the doctrine of immortality predicate a spiritual immortality. This doctrine of spiritual immortality is said to have entered Judaism ages ago under Greek influence—the Greek philosophers, notably Plato, having been exponents of that view. The Talmud contains the beautiful passage:

> The world to come has neither eating nor drinking nor mating nor commerce nor envy nor hatred nor strife; but the righteous do sit with crowns on their heads basking in the light of God's countenance (Berakot 17A).

The Talmud is fond of picturing the hereafter as an academy in which the saints continue the sacred studies which they cultivated on earth. This thought is carried to a point where it actually contradicts the idea of heaven as a place of rest. Says the Talmud: "The scholarly have rest neither in this world nor in the world to come" (Berakot 64A). Does "world to come" mean a supermundane world already existing or does it mean some future millenium on earth? Perhaps for some writers and some readers, it carried the one meaning and, for other writers and readers, the other meaning.

The Jewish prayer known as the *Kaddish* which is recited in behalf of the dead contains, in its original form, no reference to the dead. The *Kaddish* was, in its origin, a doxology, an outpouring of praise to God. Translated from the Aramaic in which most of it is couched and from the Hebrew of its terminal sentences, the Kaddish reads as follows:

Magnified and hallowed be His great name in the world which He hath created according to His will. May His kingdom come in your life and in your days and in the life of the whole house of Israel, speedily and in the near future. And say ye, Amen.

May His great name be blessed unto eternity and unto eternities of eternities.

Blessed, praised, glorified, extolled, exalted, beautified, uplifted, and lauded be the name of the Holy One, blessed be He, above all blessings and hymns, praises and consolations that are uttered in the world. And say ye, Amen.

May there be great peace from heaven, and life upon us and upon all Israel. And say ye, Amen.

The *Kaddish*, it will be seen, says nothing about the dead. Its recital was originally an act of piety in accordance with the belief that, by means of meritorious deeds, a son could shorten the term of his parent's punishment in the hereafter. The Jewish hell was not a place of eternal punishment but merely a place of temporary retribution. Not only prayer but also the study of sacred books and, above all, acts of charity on the part of the living were believed to work that beneficence for the departed. The *Kaddish* was spoken for that purpose—perhaps because it is mostly in Aramaic, and Aramaic was once the Jewish vernacular. One had to be educated in order to recite Hebrew; but there was a time when even the uneducated used Aramaic. That the attempt to advance the well-being of the dead by means of pious acts was carried to excess is evident from a thirteenth-century Jewish book of ethics which repeatedly cautions that pious acts of the living in behalf of the dead will not avail unless the dead themselves have performed meritorious deeds during their lifetime.

2. THE ATTITUDE OF JUDAISM TODAY

It was Reform Judaism which added to this doxology the reference to death and to immortality as it stands in the Union Prayer Book. That modern insertion, also Aramaic, reads:

> Upon Israel and upon the righteous and upon everyone who hath departed from this world according to the will of God, may there be great peace and a goodly portion in the life of the world to come, and mercy and compassion from the Lord of heaven and earth; and say ye, Amen.

It is this modern addition which the Union Prayer Book paraphrases in the oft-used words:

> The departed whom we now remember have entered into the peace of life eternal. They still live on earth in the acts of goodness they performed and in the hearts of those who cherish their memory. May the beauty of their lives abide among us as a loving benediction.

Exquisitely beautiful and impressive is the Memorial Service held in Reform Temples, usually on Atonement afternoon. This lovely service is permeated by the hope of life everlasting. With that import, the verse from the sixteenth Psalm is sung by the choir:

> Thou wilt not give me up to destruction:
> Nor wilt Thou suffer Thy holy one to see corruption.
> Thou wilt show me the path of life;
> In Thy presence is fulness of joy;
> At Thy right hand are pleasures forevermore.

While, except on New Year and Atonement Day, a majority of those who attend synagogue at all attend only on the anniversaries when they recite the *Kaddish* for their dear ones, it is nonetheless probable that only a minority of Jews would answer "Yes" if asked: "Do you believe in a hereafter?" The Jew is inclined toward skepticism. Most Jews who recite the prayer for the dead do so in memory or in honor of the dead without any thought that the dead survive in another world.

It is sometimes asserted that Judaism is a religion of *this* world while Christianity is a religion of the next world. That statement has been challenged, and rightly so. During the Middle Ages, the Jews were preoccupied with heaven and hell little less than were the Christians. The Talmud tells of a certain saint who lay dying. He asked to be shown the ledger in which he kept the record of his benevolences. The record indicated charitable gifts amounting to a prodigious sum. Yet the dying man sighed: "Alas, long is the journey and scant the provision!" (Ketubot 67B). The journey was the journey into the hereafter. The provision consisted in prior acts of charity, these being the great assets in the life to come. Another Talmudic passage states that the honoring of parents, acts of kindness, the furtherance of peace and, above all, the pursuit of sacred study are the deeds on which one draws interest in this world and of which one recovers the capital in the hereafter. These views are typical of the Jewish Middle Ages. The difference between Judaism and Christianity resides in the fact that Judaism, long antedating Christianity, had traversed the period before the belief in a hereafter was adopted; while, in modern times, the Jews who have discarded the belief seem to be proportionately more numerous than similar doubters in the other group.

3. MOTIVATION

Of no little religious consequence are the motives which prompt not only the affirmation of a hereafter but also its denial. Among human motivations, we must list the desire to be scientific. Those methods, by which science distinguishes between the real and the imaginery, can captivate the mind. Nonetheless, that most people, most of the time, respond to motives other than the scientific, hardly needs telling.

Among the factors operative is that of wishful thinking. One believes in a hereafter because one wishes a hereafter, and one wishes a hereafter because one shrinks from death.

Another obvious motive is that of social control. Ancient and widespread is the opinion that people can be held to desirable behavior by promises of heavenly rewards and threats of infernal punishment. Whether these doctrines wield the moral effectiveness ascribed to them has been questioned. Acceptable conduct has, in countless instances, been displayed by persons who reject these doctrines, and reprehensible conduct by people who subscribe to these doctrines. In the age when Dante wrote about heaven and hell, the belief in heaven and hell was universal. For all that, Dante depicts, as condemned to hell, hosts of his contemporaries. Modern psychological studies have similarly shown that those beliefs have surprisingly little influence on people's actions. Still, the theory is widely advocated that those beliefs facilitate social control. Social control can be a motive of the belief despite those dubious suppositions.

There is a Jewish teaching—and other religions concur—that good is to be practiced and evil avoided regardless of punishments and rewards. We have already quoted (page 42) the ancient sage who puts it: "Be not like those who serve expecting pay; be like those who serve without expecting pay." A Jewish teacher of more recent centuries words it: "The reward of a sacred act is that act itself. One should regard the very doing of a sacred act as its own recompense, and yearn for no further requital. What greater advantage does life hold than that of being a servant of God, fulfilling His holy commands?" A modern Jewish story describes the death of a saintly man. Angels from heaven and devils from hell arrive to claim the departing soul. Owing to the man's exemplary life, the devils find themselves powerless. The dying one is free to follow the angels heavenward. Yet, of his own volition, the hallowed soul decides to accompany the devils to hell. He prefers to place himself where there is anguish that he might solace and suffering that he might relieve. What an inversion of popular conceptions!

Proponents of radical economic views often impute to the belief in a hereafter a sinister intent. They charge that employers of labor foster the belief so that, counting on happiness in the world beyond, working people will submit to starvation wages and, without murmuring, endure economic exploitation. A well-known jingle thus ridicules the belief in a hereafter:

> Work and pray, live on hay;
> You'll get pie in the sky when you die.

Evidence for this accusation is scant—surely scant in our own day, even if there were any warrant for it under the shocking industrial conditions of a century or more ago. Indeed, belief in a hereafter has not rarely gone hand in hand with sincere regard for the industrial worker. Never have the working people had a friend more loyal and devoted than Henry George, the proponent of Single Tax—otherwise known as "the socialization of land." After chapter upon eloquent chapter treating such topics as capital, wages, dividends, rent, ownership, poverty, unemployment, and the like, Henry George's great masterpiece, *Progress and Poverty*, ends with a glorious disquisition on a life beyond the grave.

Considering the abundance of resentment and vindictiveness in the world, it is likely that the belief in hell may at times manifest a penchant for revenge. According to psychiatrists, one can seek revenge even against one's self. In psychiatry, we hear not a little about guilt feelings and self-punishment. The doctrine of hell-fire can serve, and probably has served, as a vent for such impulses. Correspondingly the belief in heaven can be inspired by sentiments of love. Affection can foster the wish that the loved one might remain forever untouched by death and that "there in love's undoubted reign, parted hands shall meet again." Love can also nurture the yearning to comfort the bereaved and to invoke the belief in a hereafter for that purpose. That mutualistic trait, reverence for human personality, can thus undergird the affirmation of immortality. Whatever one may judge regarding the truth or the falsity of the doctrine, fairness ever requires that we distinguish between motive and motive.

Nor need the rejection of the belief in a hereafter be a whit more scientific than its acceptance. There is in most of us—perhaps in all of us—a streak of iconoclasm and rebelliousness which, regardless of logic, instigates protest against anything conventional or official. Opposition to a belief in a hereafter often bears that feature.

4. PSYCHICAL RESEARCH

Meanwhile the all-important issue remains. How is it with us who are scientifically motivated and, at the same time, spiritually motivated? Must the two motives get in one another's way? Must we sacrifice either the promptings of science or the promptings of love as regards the question of a hereafter?

A number of considerations indicate a possible harmonization. We need not endorse the claims of Psychical Research in order to achieve this, although we must mention Psychical Research in passing. Psychical Research is the name given to the scientific study of spiritualistic mediums. Mediums have long been maintaining that their procedures furnish evidence of survival after physical death. In the presence of a number of persons seated around a table, the medium goes into a trance, or a pretended trance, during which there occur what purport to be communications from the deceased. Those supposed communications sometimes take the form of automatic slatewriting, sometimes the form of words or sentences spelled out by a planchette, and sometimes the form of audible knockings preconcertedly signifying the various letters of the alphabet. We are told that, on occasion, apparitions emerge which resemble certain of the departed. A notable literary description of a mediumistic séance is to be found in Thomas Mann's novel, *The Magic Mountain*. Most people take it for granted that these demonstrations are partly fraud and partly hallucination. Nevertheless, they have attracted the study of such men as Sir

Oliver Lodge, William James, Thomas A. Edison, Sir Arthur Conan Doyle, James Hyslop, William T. Stead, F. W. H. Myers, and others. These scientific investigators testify that, even granting the presence of fraud and hallucination, there remains a certain residue which cannot be accounted for in that way. In fact, the science of Psychical Research consists chiefly of measures for exposing fraud and detecting hallucination. Some of the psychical researchers report that they have come upon happenings which cannot possibly be comprehended under any other hypothesis than that of personal survival.

The array of notable scientific men who have devoted time to the study of mediumistic performances inspires respect for Psychical Research. The vitiating circumstance lurks in the fact that Psychical Research has never ceased to be a pursuit limited to a venturesome few. No university in the world has, as yet, established a chair of Psychical Research. The psychological and psychiatric associations never list a paper on Psychical Research in the programs of their conferences. Those of us to whom the field is strange cannot but keep our judgment in abeyance until this lack of vitality in the Psychical Research movement has been explained. All that we can say with assurance is that men of great eminence and great probity have staked their reputations on the contention that mediumism contains something besides mere fraud or self-deception.

5. THE DIFFICULTIES OF NEGATING

A more cautious approach would consist in noticing not the affirmation of a hereafter but its negation. Whatever the difficulties of affirming a hereafter, the difficulties of negating are insuperable. To deny a hereafter is to say: "Beyond death, nothing," "Beyond death, extinction," "Beyond death, non-existence." But do those words convey any ideas? When we say: "There is nothing in that box" do we really mean "nothing?" After all, there is air in the box or there is a vacuum or there are particles of dust drifting around in the box or there is the quadrangle formed by the inner sides of the box. When we say that there is nothing in the box, we mean that there is *something* in the box, but something different from what we need or want. Such is the import of all terms of negation, absence, non-existence. Such terms convey not the absence of everything but the presence of *something* other than what evokes our interest. That there can be a "nothing," there has to be a "something." "Beyond death, nothing" is either meaningless or it means the opposite of what the speaker intends it to mean. It means: "Beyond death, something."

Still more meaningless is the sentence: "The belief in a hereafter is false." That sentence is self-contradictory. It is as if one were to say: "That circle is four-cornered," "That water is dry," "The part is larger than the whole." Falsehood means disappointment of expectation. A statement leads us to expect some future occurrence. If events turn out as expected, the statement is true. If they turn out otherwise than as expected, the statement is false. Falsehood implies always a later experience in which expectation is thwarted. The only way in which the belief in a hereafter could be false would be by means of a hereafter in which the expectation of a hereafter would fail of fulfilment. Can self-contradiction go any further?

The affirmation of a hereafter is distinctly free of those difficulties. When it comes to imagining a hereafter, phantasy is never baffled. Dante's *Divine Comedy* and that Jewish book, *Hell and Paradise*, by Immanuel of Rome ,1270-1330), are but two examples. Those phantasies may be erroneous. Yet such phantasies are possible. Such phantasies do exist. Particularly helpful in this connection is the phenomenon of dreaming. There is a dream world and there is a real world. The two have some strains in common, and yet those worlds are detached from one another. One can think of our present life as a dream from which bodily death could mark an awakening. Sometimes this life is a nightmare. Its termination might be attended by a profound sense of relief such as comes over us when, awakening from a terror-fraught vision, we exclaim: "Thank God, it was a dream, nothing more!" If one needs an analogy by means of which to conceive the transition from this life to a hereafter, the dream phenomenon might furnish the model. The analogy might even aid us to understand why, assuming the mediums to be wrong, no one has ever returned from the dead or communicated from the dead. Between dream and reality, transportation or communication cannot obtain. In brief, imagery for a life beyond is not wanting. The same cannot be said for the contrary view.

Yes, the remark that "No one has ever returned" gives negation little support. The universe abounds in that which never returns. The past never returns. Once succeeded by maturity, youth never returns. Anything that goes up in flames never returns. The full-grown tree never reverts to the sapling. All of us have seen freakish moving pictures which show the breaking of a vessel or the dynamiting of an edifice and then render the same performance in reverse, the vessel recovering its former state and the edifice resuming its previous structure. These curious pictures only illustrate the non-returning character of much that transpires. The non-return of the dead bears neither one way nor the other on the question of a hereafter.

6. MIND AND BODY

The chief impediment to affirming a hereafter lies in the close connection between mind and body. All mentation is physiological. The brain, indeed the entire nervous system, is indispensable for feeling, thinking, willing. What we call mind consists of bodily processes sometimes more subtle, sometimes less subtle. We cannot think "mind" without thinking "body." It seems to follow that, when body disintegrates, mind also must come to an end.

This conclusion, however, is not inevasible. Modern physics and chemistry have discovered forms of matter which have hitherto escaped all human surmise. The most recent example is atomic energy. Just as certain forms of matter are known today which were unknown previously, there is no telling what additional forms of matter the universe might include. How amazed and incredulous the people of the Middle Ages would have been had someone told them about the telegraph, the telephone, the automobile, the radio, television, X-ray, jet propulsion, aviation, and the rest! Does this not prove that it is possible for forms of matter to exist whereof people possess no intimation? Similarly there could be an invisible physique which survives when the visible organism crumbles.

Such would, in fact, comport with a well known biological process. The body is not a lump of matter but a stream of matter. Old cells are constantly being sloughed off; new cells are constantly being added. We are told that, in our bodies today, there is not one atom of matter which was there a number of years ago. New matter is constantly superseding old matter. Would the process be altogether different if, at the body's death, invisible matter would take over when visible matter defaults? In a sense, one's body is dying constantly, and still we survive.

This invites another analogy—namely, that of a person who writes for publication. An author begins by scrawling a first draft. Afterward he prepares a second draft greatly improving upon the first. As the second draft takes form, the first is thrown to the waste. Later a third draft, better than the second, supplants the second. There may follow a fourth or a fifth or a sixth draft. Each draft improves upon its predecessor, and each draft lands in the waste-basket as its successor develops. The composition itself outlives the successive drafts and progresses with the successive drafts. Using this analogy, we can imagine a discarded visible body supplanted by a subsequent invisible body, while the personality itself survives from the one to the other.

Survival beyond the grave would, we grant, be something wonderful, amazing, incredible. But what is there in the universe which is not wonderful, amazing, incredible? Is not matter, in its everyday manifestations, miraculous? The survival of mind under non-mundane conditions would be in no wise more astounding than is mind as we know it to exist in conjunction with the familiar bodily processes.

7. CONCLUSION

The general tenor of existence is likewise of profound relevance here—that intermingling and alternation of good and evil, joy and sorrow which is, for us, the meaning of God (page 22). Why must death fall out of the universal rhythm? Why need the evil of death fail to be followed by some corresponding good? A hereafter would exemplify but another instance of that redemption which prevails throughout our experience.

Still, one might rejoin: "Say what you will, at best a hereafter is fraught with uncertainty." But the words "certainty" and "uncertainty" refer to the present physical world. The things about which we are either certain or uncertain are, all of them, matters of bodily perception and cognition. To speak of certainty or uncertainty with regard to anything outside of bodily perception and cognition were like asking whether a polygon is male or female, whether a glow-worm is democratic or republican, whether a musical octave is hot or cold. Our language becomes inapplicable. Anything subject to the distinction between certain and uncertain could not possibly lie outside of the world which is now and here. It has to be something which engages our present brain and nervous system. With regard to a hereafter, "certain" and "uncertain" amount to empty words.

These remarks, let us recall, are addressed neither to those who assert a hereafter nor to those who deny. They are intended for those who crave a hereafter and, at the same time, respect the scientific point of view. Our conclusion is that we can remain unswervingly loyal to the spirit of science and still recognize that the negation of a hereafter brims with difficulties.

As our Bible itself illustrates, religion at its best is possible without raising the issue of a life beyond. Superb values have been religionized (page 17) without the religionizing of the belief in immortality. Nonetheless, once the issue arises, once a choice becomes imperative, affirmation and not negation appears to approach the nearer to the truth.

CHAPTER TEN

Maturity

ABOUT MATURITY and immaturity, modern psychology and psychiatry have much to say. An example of this reached us in our chapter on War and Peace (page 103). Our quotation read:

> Human beings usually function on two levels: one mature and rational, the other infantile and egocentric. It's the basically childish attitude of seeing other people as potential rivals and sources of danger that arouses that hostility which leads to wars.

In psychiatric literature, these references to the childish abound.

Infancy is charming; childhood is lovable. Were it otherwise, the human race would hardly have developed. But qualities, entrancing in a youngster, become appalling if they persist into later life. A person, mature in years, can be a child intellectually. One can be mature intellectually, yet swayed by infantile emotions. Maladjustments in marriage, in employment, in education, in citizenship have been traced to the retardation by which people, adult as to birthdays, are far from adult in other particulars. An excellent book on the subject of marriage advises that people should not marry unless they are old enough to marry. The book then proceeds to explain that it means not merely old enough as to years but, more than that, old enough intellectually and emotionally. If the husband is a baby or the wife a baby in that sense, the prospects of an enduring marriage are dubious.

1. SIGNS OF IMMATURITY

A familiar symptom of immaturity is hypersensitiveness. The immature person carries, as we say, "a chip on the shoulder." He complains of slights. Frequent are his protests that the deference shown him is not enough. He is not noticed enough, respected enough, admired enough. That person has not outgrown the baby's clamor for attention.

The immature person is fond of being praised. Praise transports him, and bitter anguish assails him when expected praise is not forthcoming. Also among the infantile qualities which sometimes continue through the years are peevishness, quarrelsomeness, and vindictiveness. Affectation and ostentation likewise belong to that state, and likewise airs of importance.

The child worries little about the distinction between fact and fiction. A child's thinking is wishful thinking; with the child, the true and the imaginary merge. Maturity, by contrast, craves realism. Maturity discriminates punctiliously between the actual and the fancied.

The concern for reality has varied manifestations. One of them consists in devotion to the viewpoint of science. The hallmark of science is precise definition of terms, careful and protracted observation, accurate measuring, meticulous recording, rigid testing. An individual may not command the leisure or the training to apply the scientific technique to all situations. But an individual will, if mature, lack no alertness in raising the question: "Is that statement proved or unproved? Is it unverified or scientifically verified?"

The distinction between the real and the unreal includes the distinction between our reasons and our rationalizations (page 54). A mature person scrutinizes all arguments, even his own, knowing how often a fictitious reason masks the true reason. When the mature person hears that the function of capital punishment is that of preventing murder, he may stop and inquire whether the real function may not be retaliation. When apprised that certain rituals commend themselves by their beauty, he may wish to query whether their real commendation may not lurk in the sense of worthiness which they impart to their performer. When told that a certain doctrine is supported by Scripture, he may pause to ask whether that doctrine may not derive its real support from the fact that it is easier to reiterate old thoughts than to evolve new thoughts. Against rationalization, the mature person stands guard.

The mature person knows that life brings reverses as well as triumphs. Calamity does not daze him as something incredible. The immature person is, by contrast, dumbfounded that anything untoward should ever befall. To the immature person, it is altogether natural and normal that adversities should descend upon others; but that he himself should encounter affliction is, to the immature person, incomprehensible. The immature person lives in a paradise of phantasy. This pertains, above all, to the individual's own person and accomplishments. The mature person realizes that he cannot always excel, cannot always lead, cannot always march in the forefront. The immature person does not grasp this. The immature person deems it unbelievable that he should possess ever a flaw. The mature person is well aware that there is a limit to every excellence; he has accordingly learned to reckon with his imperfections. If fault is found with him, he is not crushed. There is perhaps nothing which so sharply marks the difference between immaturity and maturity as the individual's reaction to adverse criticism. To the immature, adverse criticism is intolerable. Admitting that he has made a mistake is, for the immature person, unendurable. For the immature person, it is indispensable always to be in the right.

An outstanding difference between the mature and the immature asserts itself in the matter of blaming. A noted psychologist observes that no one is a hopeless failure so long as he does not blame his setbacks upon others. There are reasons for suspecting that such acts as blaming, scolding, denouncing rest invariably upon the blurring of reality with fiction. We discern this every time we are ourselves the object of reproach. How uninformed is our denouncer! How he misses the salient facts and circumstances of the deed which he condemns! If this prevails when we are the ones who suffer rebuke, why need it be otherwise when we are the rebukers? A few illustrations will clarify the thought:

A woman stopping in an immense hotel grew more and more exasperated as the elevator for which she was ringing failed to arrive. When, at long last, the elevator did arrive, the woman heaped the operator with abuse. The woman would not have done this had she known the facts. A crippled old veteran, on a higher floor, had needed assistance to get from the elevator to his room. There was none except the elevator operator to extend the help. That was why the elevator was delayed. Ignorance of the facts caused the woman's angry outburst.

A large number of people were crowding into a train. A man in the throng berated the man in front of him for blocking the way. The scolder did not see that, in front of the man he was upbraiding, some small children were being helped into the coach. To avoid blocking the way the censured man would have had to trample on the little ones. The scolder would not have scolded had he known the facts.

Many years ago, there lived in New York City a well known, much loved Yiddish poet, Morris Rosenfeld. In his old age, Rosenfeld was stricken with paralysis. A committee was formed to raise a sum of money on which the afflicted poet could subsist during his last years. Contributions to the fund came from friends and admirers all over the world.

Soon after the fund was completed, Rosenfeld was violently attacked by a certain Jewish newspaper. "Think of it," exclaimed the paper, "Rosenfeld accepted the money raised for him although he owns an apartment house from which he draws lucrative rentals. Rosenfeld is an imposter. He is a deceiver. He is a shrewd trickster."

Here again ignorance of the facts underlay the censure. Rosenfeld did indeed own an apartment house. He did derive rentals from that apartment house. But the apartment house had been purchased *for* Rosenfeld with those very funds which his friends had collected. The committee had judged that the wisest way in which to aid the poet was by means of a sound investment yielding a regular income. There would have been no attack on Rosenfeld had the newspaper known the facts.

Let one more example suffice:

In a moving picture theatre, during the recent war, the entire audience stood up to sing "The Star Spangled Banner." Much to the irritation of the bystanders, one man remained seated. Some excessively patriotic individuals in the audience proceeded to punish the man for his remissness. The man was rudely flung off his seat. Then the reason for his dereliction was discovered. The man had no legs. He was an American veteran who had lost his legs at the Normandy landing in June, 1944. Knowing the facts makes a world of difference.

There is nothing exceptional about these cases. They are typical. A French proverb puts it aptly: "To comprehend all is to pardon all." Spinoza once remarked that we are never exasperated by any act of human conduct whereof we have traced the causes. This applies not only when the object of the scolding is an individual but equally when the object is a group—Catholics, Jews, Communists, Negroes, Capitalists, "Big Business," "Wall Street," "Labor Bosses"—any class that may be under attack. This surely applies when reproof is hurled at a nation. It has become almost proverbial, as we have already noticed (page 102), that, in any war, truth is the first casualty.

Children are often accused of lying. It were more correct to say that children cannot see the boundary between the actual and the fancied. The person addicted to exaggeration or distortion is simply one who has failed to grow up.

This does not deny that there are evils in the world and that those evils need correcting. But there is a childish way of handling evils and a mature way. All that the child understands is to hit and to wail. The child knows nothing about inquiry and research. The methods of the physician who does not berate the illness and does not pummel the illness but who diagnoses it and who applies the findings of medical science—such are the methods of maturity. There is a Chinese proverb: "Do not curse the dark; light a candle." That difference is the difference between the child and the adult. Vilification, sarcasm, vituperation are the earmarks of unresourcefulness, that is, of immaturity.

A child never follows through with any fixed goal. Whatever a child undertakes is speedily interrupted by the encroachments of other things upon the child's attention. The opposite characterizes maturity. The mature person perceives his objective and adheres to his objective. The mature person separates the non-essential from the essential. He is not trapped by the superficial. Frills and fanfares do not deflect him. Tinsel and glitter do not dazzle him. Sensational and spectacular methods must justify themselves, for the mature person, not by the momentary excitement they provide but by the extent to which they advance their professed purposes. If we expect of a religious organization that it contribute to the improvement of human relationships, its failure to promote such improvement finds, with the mature person, no compensation in the size of the organization, its publicity, its photography, its slogans, or any other form of "ballyhoo." A picket line may thrill, but a mature person needs more than thrills. He asks: "What does that picket line accomplish for those striking workers or for those under-privileged Negroes?" Political invective may entertain and even amuse; but the mature person seeks political insight. All of these are ways in which the mature person draws the line between the unreal and the real.

A child is considerate only of itself. A mature person is considerate of others. A child accepts its parents' gifts and attentions without an inkling of the toil and the sacrifice which those gifts and attentions have cost. A mature person understands people's labors and renunciations. While making few demands for himself, the mature person is generous in his appreciation of others and his recognition of others. A child knows nothing about obligation;

that concept eludes its ken. The mature person is, by contrast, a responsible person. A promise made is a promise to be kept. A mature person pays his debts with promptness. Money-lenders are keenly aware of the infantilism which borrows and then forgets the transaction. Anything loaned to a mature person is returned without needless delay. A mature person is punctual. A mature person is reliable. What he is depended upon to do, he does. Somebody once offered a humorous definition of the word "organization." "An organization," he quipped, "is a group of people in which everybody expects someone else to do the work." The mature person sees to it that he himself does the work assigned him or accepted by him. The mature person does not shift his responsibilities.

Religion has often been criticized for its encouragement of infantilism. Infantilism has indeed been religionized at various times and places, particularly in the religious stressing of submission, obedience, and conformity, as well as in the religious penchant for denunciation and the religious prepossessions about reward and punishment. Yet there have been other times and places which have religionized maturity. We ourselves assuredly stand prepared to religionize maturity.

2. THE JEWISH PHASE

Is maturity Jewish? Once more we must recall the varied senses in which the term "Jewish" is employed (page 47). The term is often one of commendation. Many of us apply it to traits, objects, or actions that we wish to praise. Examples of such are: "A noble character is Jewish," "Devoted home-life is Jewish," "Love of justice is Jewish." Alongside of this usage, there is the other usage, the usage by which certain people, institutions, books, or practices are labeled. Examples would be: "The six-point shield is a Jewish symbol," "The ram's horn is a Jewish ceremonial object," "The Jewish population of America exceeds five million."

Maturity is indeed Jewish if we employ "Jewish" in the former sense. If "Jewish" is, with us, a term of encomium, and maturity a trait which we applaud, then is maturity Jewish *ipso facto*. We deliberately make it Jewish.

Maturity is, at the same time, Jewish in that other sense of the word. The ideal of maturity attained moving expression in the Jewish books of long ago. We of today would cherish maturity even if it had not been extolled in the Jewish books. That it has been thus extolled should make us appreciative and grateful. In our own quest for maturity, our literary masterpieces can be of priceless aid.

We can instance, first of all, those immortal expressions of longing for the Infinite and the Eternal:

> As the stag panteth after the water-brooks,
> So panteth my soul after Thee, O God.
> My soul thirsteth for God, for the living God (Psalm 42.2, 3).

> Whom have I in heaven but Thee?
> And beside Thee, I desire none upon earth.
> My flesh and my heart faileth:
> But God is the rock of my heart and my portion for ever . . .
> The nearness of God is my good (Psalm 73.25, 26, 28).

> My soul waiteth for the Lord
> More than watchmen for the morning (Psalm 130.6).

> In the Lord God is the Rock of Ages (Isaiah 26.4).

> "The Lord is my portion," saith my soul,
> "Therefore will I hope in Him." (Lamentations 3.24).

> May we awaken in the morning to find our heart's hope in the revering of Thy name and our soul's serenity in Thy blessed presence (Berakot 16B).

What a severance from the trivial and the superficial! The sensational and the spectacular—how they are renounced! Underlying these expressions of yearning for God, one senses—and correctly senses—non-competitiveness in human attitudes (page 43). The rock-bottom reality lies in felicitous human relationships; and precisely these are the values manifest—even when not verbally mentioned—in the upreach for God. Is not this the very quintessence of maturity?

The biblical selection which is perhaps the best known piece of literature in the world, does it not also incarnate maturity, with its calm, its clarity, its insight? There is nothing infantile about the twenty-third Psalm:

The Lord is my shepherd; I shall not want.
He maketh me to lie down in green pastures;
He leadeth me beside the still waters.
He restoreth my soul;
He guideth me in straight paths for His name's sake.
Yea, though I walk through the valley of the shadow of death,
I will fear no evil,
For Thou art with me;
Thy rod and Thy staff, they comfort me . . .
Surely goodness and mercy shall follow me all the days
    of my life;
And I shall dwell in the house of the Lord for ever.

Out of the depths of human experience, Judaism has come to say "Heavenly Father." The correlative of Heavenly Father is not human childishness. The correlative is human maturity. "Heavenly Father" implies not juvenile conduct on our part but the conduct of the full-grown. A passage from the Talmud will make this vivid. The passage relates to the calamities amid which the Judean state came to an end more than eighteen hundred years ago:

Since the Temple was destroyed, the free and the scholarly are shamed, the active fail in strength, the violent and the talkative hold sway. None ponders, none seeks, none inquires. Upon whom shall we rely? Upon our Father who is in heaven.

Since the Temple was destroyed, sages have descended to the rank of tutors, tutors have become like housemen, housemen like the untaught, and the untaught have sunk deeper and deeper. None ponders, none seeks, none inquires. Upon whom shall we rely? Upon our Father who is in heaven.

Ere the Messiah comes, impudence will increase and vainglory run rampant (nobles become oppressive). Though grapes will abound, the cost of wine will soar. Government will become subverted, and none will protest. The house of assembly will become a house of fornication. Galilee will be devastated, Gablan lie desolate. The people of the frontier will wander from place to place and find no compassion. The wisdom of the learned will decay. Those who shrink from sin will be contemned. Truth will vanish. The young will disrespect the old. Elders will have to stand up before youngsters. The son will dishonor the father, the daughter rise up against the mother, the daughter-in-law against the mother-in-law. The members of a man's household will be his foes. The look of the generation will be the look of a dog. The son will feel no shame in the presence of his sire. Upon whom shall we rely? Upon our Father who is in heaven (Sotah IX, 15).

There is nothing here of a child's utopia. The passage comes to grips with reality at its hardest.

Saturated with maturity are the eloquent Jewish clauses which warn against loquacity. A human being learns how to talk long before he learns how to refrain from talk. The child, just beginning to speak, babbles incessantly. Concerning the blessedness of silence, the Jewish sages evince captivating wisdom:

Only for God doth my soul wait in stillness . . .
Only for God wait thou in stillness, my soul (Psalm 62.1, 5).

Say little, do much (Abot I, 15).

Much talk brings sin (Abot I, 17).

I have found nothing better for a person than silence (Abot I, 17).

A fence to wisdom is silence (Abot III, 17).

Too numerous for counting are the occurrences of such words as "kindness," "truth," and "peace" in the Bible as well as in the books of the Rabbis:

Let not kindness and truth forsake thee (Proverbs 3.3).

By mercy and truth, iniquity is atoned for (Proverbs 16.6).

Mercy and truth are met together:
Righteousness and peace have kissed each other (Psalm 85.11).

Execute the judgment of truth and peace . . .
Love ye truth and peace (Zechariah 8.16, 19).

Truth is the signet of God (Sabbath 55A).

A sage of old asked five of his disciples: "Which is the way to be cherished as good?" One answered: "Freedom from envy." Another answered: "A good friend." Another: "A good neighbor." Another: "Foresight." The last replied: "A good heart." "That last answer," said the teacher, "has my preference. It includes all the others" (Abot II, 13).

Kindness, truth, and peace are not the qualities of infants. Before one can be kind, truthful, and effective for peace, one has to be mature.

When it comes to heeding the prophet's admonition to do justly, to love mercy, and to walk humbly (Micah 6.8), none except the mature is capable. Note humility in particular. Immaturity and humility exclude one another.

Lord, my heart is not haughty, nor mine eyes lofty; neither do I exercise myself in things too great, or in things too wonderful for me (Psalm 131.1).

With the lowly is wisdom (Proverbs 11.2).

Better it is to be of a lowly spirit with the humble
Than to divide spoil with the proud (Proverbs 16.19).

Be thou, to the utmost, lowly (Abot IV, 4).

A humble and lowly spirit betokens the disciple of Abraham
(Abot V, 22).

Let my soul be as the dust before all (Berakot 17A).

All of this calls for maturity. When the Talmud teaches, "Envy, cupidity, and ambition put one out of the world" (Abot IV, 28), it is features of immaturity that are singled out for disparagement.

What we have observed about the mature person's aptitude for suspecting rationalization comports with the words of Jeremiah (17.9):

> The heart is deceitful above all things,
> And it is exceedingly weak—who can know it?

Nor do the sacred books ignore the significance of paying one's debts. Psalm 37.21 reads: "The wicked borroweth and payeth not." The "wicked" is, in modern parlance, the person who is poorly adjusted; and the poorly adjusted person is the one whose maturity lags behind the numeration of his years.

Not far removed from our comment about the childishness of blaming and scolding are Rabbinic adages such as these:

> When judging people, use the scale of merit (Abot I, 6).

> Judge not thy neighbor until thou art come into his place (Abot II, 5).

> First correct thyself, then correct others (Sanhedrin 18A).

and, above all, that striking Talmudic aphorism: "Retribution will overtake the accuser before it overtakes the accused" (Baba Kama 93A).

The Book of Ecclesiastes holds that "anger resteth in the bosom of fools" (7.9). The Book of Leviticus (19.18) admonishes: "Thou shalt not take vengeance, nor bear any grudge." A famous adage of Hillel reads: "If I look not out for myself, who will look out for me?" (Abot I, 14). The traits here commended are all of them inseparable from maturity.

Especially impressive is the saying of Ben-Zoma, a Jewish sage who lived in the first part of the second Christian century:

> Who is mighty? He who subdues his own passions.
> Who is rich? He who rejoices in what he has.
> Who is honored? He who honors others (Abot IV, 1).

Immaturity knows not any heroism except that of brute force. Immaturity knows not any riches except that of material possessions. It knows not any honor except that of winning flattery. Ben-Zoma was right. The greatest honor we can achieve consists not in the honors we get but in our readiness to honor others. All of which is more than the immature can envision.

Another sage taught: "Love to work, hate to domineer" (Abot I, 10). Immaturity loves to domineer and hates to work. Immaturity is like the bramble in the ninth chapter of the Book of Judges. When the trees wanted a king, the olive-tree declined. "Should I leave my fatness . . . " said the olive-tree, "and hold sway over the trees?" The fig-tree also declined. "Should I leave my sweetness . . . " he remarked, "and hold sway over the trees?" The grapevine likewise declined. "Should I leave my wine . . . " he asked, "and hold sway over the trees?" The bramble accepted. The bramble shouted: "Let fire come out of the bramble and devour the cedars."

Thus, from the Jewish writings, we cull those passages which propound maturity. Even aside from these, we identify our own Judaism with maturity. Maturity synopsizes most of what has been urged in these Jewish thoughts for Jewish youth. It embraces most of what we would religionize. Maturity represents a consummate form of redemption (page 22)—inner redemption, spiritual redemption. And maturity is attained less by our own efforts than by the impact of experience. Maturity is thus, in a singular sense, a gift of Divine grace. Maturity signifies, as naught else signifies, our upreach for God. Maturity constitutes our truest anchorage in God.

Index